Collins

11+

Comprehension and Spelling, Punctuation & Grammar

Support & Practice Workbook

Louise Swann, Hilary Male and Chris Pearse

Published by Collins
An imprint of HarperCollins*Publishers* Ltd
1 London Bridge Street
London SE1 9GF

HarperCollins*Publishers*
Macken House
39/40 Mayor Street Upper
Dublin 1
D01 C9W8
Ireland

ISBN 978-0-00-856258-8

First published 2023

10 9 8 7 6 5 4 3 2

British Library Cataloguing in Publication Data.
A CIP record of this book is available from the British Library.

Publisher: Clare Souza
Authors: Louise Swann, Hilary Male and Chris Pearse
Project Management and Editorial: Richard Toms and Tracey Cowell
Cover Design: Kevin Robbins and Sarah Duxbury
Inside Concept Design, Typesetting and Artwork: Ian Wrigley
Production: Emma Wood

Published in collaboration with Teachitright.
Billy the Bookworm™ is the property of Teachitright Ltd.

Printed in the United Kingdom

Contents

Introduction

Teachitright

This book has been published in collaboration with Teachitright, one of the most successful 11+ tuition companies in the South-East. Teachitright has supported thousands of children for both grammar school and independent school entry. It has several tuition centres across the UK, including Berkshire, Buckinghamshire, Surrey and the West Midlands.

With considerable experience and knowledge, Teachitright has produced a range of books to support children through their 11+ journey for GL Assessment, CEM and many Common Entrance exams. The books have been written by qualified teachers, tested in the classroom with pupils, and adapted to ensure children are fully prepared and able to perform to the best of their ability.

Teachitright's unique mascot, Billy the Bookworm, helps to guide children through this book and gives helpful hints and tips along the way. We hope your child finds this book useful and informative and we wish them luck on their 11+ journey.

Teachitright holds a number of comprehensive revision courses and mock exams throughout the year. For more information, visit **www.teachitright.com**

Comprehension Exercises

This book uses a variety of different types of question and these are outlined in the table below.

Type of question	How to locate the answer
Factual questions	These questions require the answer to be extracted directly from the text.
Inference questions	The answer will not be stated directly in the passage but can be solved by using clues in the extract. This involves reading between the lines.
Personal opinion questions	Using evidence in the extract, the reader can form a personal judgement and opinion about the text.
Grammar, literacy devices and vocabulary questions	Knowledge of grammar and literacy devices (e.g. alliteration) and a wide vocabulary base are needed to answer these questions. The answers will not be stated directly in the text.

The five steps below will help children to work through each comprehension exercise.

1. Read the passage first and try to understand what the text is saying.
2. Do not skim-read the passage as important parts may be missed, and links between the concepts often need to be made.
3. Underlining key words or phrases can help in understanding and retaining the key points. Excessive underlining should be avoided as it may cause confusion and take up valuable time.
4. After thoroughly reading the passage, move on to the questions and refer back to the text to help find the answers. Line references given in some of the questions will direct children to the relevant parts of the passage.
5. Double check that all questions have been answered and, if time allows, go back and read the passage for a second time.

Children should indicate their answers to the comprehension questions in this book by marking a horizontal line through the green box beside their chosen option. They will have to mark answers in this way in the actual exam:

| The **right** way to mark your answers on the answer sheet in the exam.

 is the **right** way | The **wrong** way to mark your answers on the answer sheet in the exam.

 is the **wrong** way   is the **wrong** way

is the **wrong** way   is the **wrong** way |

Spelling, Punctuation and Grammar Sections

Spelling

Having a good understanding of spelling rules and being able to recognise homophones are important skills in these questions. Within a sentence, your child should try to identify one spelling mistake and select option A, B, C or D for the group of words in which it occurs. If there are no errors, they should select the letter 'N'.

Keeping a record of the more challenging words and revising them nearer the examination date will help.

Punctuation

These sections involve reading a sentence to spot a punctuation error or a missing piece of punctuation. Again, your child should choose option A, B, C or D to show where the error occurs. If there are no errors, they should select the letter 'N'.

Children need to know the functions of the different punctuation marks, chiefly the following:

Punctuation mark		Function
!	exclamation mark	Used to show someone shouting or giving a command; it can also show strong feelings like fear, anger or surprise
,	comma	Used to separate parts of a sentence and items in a list
'	apostrophe	Used to show possession or the contraction of words
?	question mark	Used only for sentences that ask a question
( )	brackets	Used around extra information to keep it separate from the rest of the sentence
—	dash	Another device that can be used to separate information from the rest of the sentence
" "	speech marks	Used to quote direct speech – the actual words someone speaks
:	colon	Used to show that a list or speech is about to begin
;	semi-colon	Used to break up lists, long phrases or clauses
-	hyphen	Used to help clarify meaning of words, e.g. *re-cover* as opposed to *recover*
…	ellipsis	Used when deliberately leaving a sentence unfinished, perhaps to add suspense to a story

Grammar

In the grammar questions, children are asked to choose a word or phrase to complete a sentence. Your child should select A, B, C, D or E to indicate the best option.

Children should read the whole sentence carefully and use their understanding of grammatical rules. Learning different word types will support them in these questions.

Mark Scheme and Recording Results

The answers for all questions can be found at the back of the book, along with explanations where appropriate. A marking chart and a progress grid help to keep a record of scores achieved.

Online Video Tutorial

An online video tutorial to help with technique is available at **www.collins.co.uk/11plusresources**

COMPREHENSION AND SPELLING,

PUNCTUATION & GRAMMAR 1

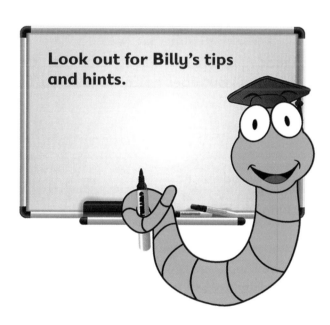

LEARN: WORD TYPES

Most comprehension tasks will ask you to understand and identify different word types that are used in the passage.

Adjectives

An adjective is a word that describes a noun, such as a *green* door.

Watch out for adjectives that may seem to be verbs at first glance, but are actually present or past participles of verbs (ending in *-ing*, *-ed* or *-en*) that become adjectives.

> ### Example question 1
>
> Which word in this sentence is an adjective?
>
> The vibrating machine appeared about to explode at any moment.

Adverbs

An adverb is a word used to modify a verb, an adjective or even another adverb. It often ends in *-ly* (such as 'She was clearly tiring') but does not always do so. Similarly, not every word that ends in *-ly* is an adverb.

> ### Example question 2
>
> Which word in this sentence is an adverb?
>
> Organisation was sadly lacking at the class play.

Nouns

A noun is a naming word. It is a thing, a person, an animal or a place. There are many different types of nouns.

- **Proper nouns**

  A proper noun is the name of a person or a place, such as Ria or London. Proper nouns always start with a capital letter.

- **Common nouns**

  A common noun describes an object or thing and does not have a capital letter, such as a bicycle or curtains.

- **Concrete nouns**

  A concrete noun is an object or thing that you can physically touch, such as a chair or vase or elephant. Concrete nouns include common nouns and most proper nouns.

- **Abstract nouns**

  An abstract noun is a thing that you cannot physically touch, such as education, imagination or failure.

Example question 3

In this sentence, what type of noun is 'hope'?

Peter was full of hope that his exam results would be good.

Example question 4

In this sentence, what type of noun is 'Germany'?

When I went on holiday, I visited Germany.

Prepositions

A preposition is a word that links a sentence to explain where things are in time or space, such as 'before', 'over' or 'under'.

Example question 5

Which word in this sentence is a preposition?

The police started moving towards the disturbance.

Word type questions always come up in comprehensions. Practise identifying as many words as possible in your own time.

COMPREHENSION

15:00
15 minutes

Read the passage below and then answer the questions that follow.

A Letter Home

1 Dearest Mother

I have now been in the trenches for a whole month. It isn't as bad as some people make out; there is plenty of protection from the enemy shells, we get regular food and once a week the post arrives!

5 Talking of which, I did appreciate the parcel you sent me last week. The chaps were very jealous of my new shaving brush! Did you get it from Mr Johnson's local store, I wonder? I am sure I saw one just like it before I left for France.

Anyway, I am not allowed to tell you about our operations in my letters as they will get censored and you will not have much to read! So please don't expect me to keep you
10 informed on that front, it will need to be *The Times* for that.

I have met some delightful chaps here. There is even someone from West London like me! His name is Taylor, but he prefers the name Davy for some reason, so that is what we call him. I think you would like him a lot, dearest Mother.

Davy is such wonderful company. He is a gardener in England and he works the stately
15 homes of the rich and famous. Have you heard of the Earl of Rochester? Davy says he is worth over a million pounds and his home employs nearly fifty servants. Anyway, he told me a story that he was asked to mow their lawns one summer and it took him nearly a week to get it all done. I kept thinking of your little garden, Mother, where you barely have room for your deckchair. How the other half live, eh?

20 I do hope you are keeping well. How are you going with the ration book? I suppose without me and Sid there you don't have to buy quite as much bacon and eggs, but I know how fond Dad is of his food so I hope that you are still getting your fair share. Davy tells me that he has heard there are dreadful shortages in London at the moment. I do hope you are not struggling.

25 I must end this letter as I am soon to go on watch. I have to guard the trench for six hours so it is important I get a little sleep before that. I do miss you Mother and can't wait for my leave when I can come home and see you.

Love

Robert

1. **Why is Robert in France?**
   - A   He has gone there on holiday.
   - B   It is impossible to tell.
   - C   He is fighting in a war.
   - D   He is working as a gardener.
   - E   He is teaching English to French students.

2. **Why did Robert think the trenches weren't that bad?**
   - A   The experience was actually enjoyable.
   - B   They got fed, were protected and got post.
   - C   The experience was exciting.
   - D   The letter doesn't say.
   - E   They got fed and were protected by the posts.

3. **What type of word is 'stately' in line 14?**
   - A   Adjective
   - B   Noun
   - C   Verb
   - D   Adverb
   - E   Preposition

4. **Where did Robert's mother get the shaving brush from?**
   - A   She got it from a friend.
   - B   Her husband gave it to her.
   - C   She bought it from Mr Johnson's local store.
   - D   She swapped it for her ration book.
   - E   The letter doesn't say.

5. **Why would Robert's letters have been censored?**
   - A   To improve their spelling
   - B   To make sure Robert wasn't revealing any war secrets
   - C   To advertise roles in the army
   - D   So there isn't as much to read
   - E   So they could be shown in Mr Johnson's store

(6) **What would *The Times* have been?**

- [ ] **A** A clock
- [ ] **B** The television news
- [ ] **C** A newspaper
- [ ] **D** A local gossip magazine
- [ ] **E** The army dispatches

(7) **Where was Davy from?**

- [ ] **A** France
- [ ] **B** Rochester
- [ ] **C** East London
- [ ] **D** West London
- [ ] **E** Scotland

(8) **Why would it have taken Davy 'nearly a week' (line 17) to mow the lawns?**

- [ ] **A** Because he lived so far away
- [ ] **B** Because of poor equipment
- [ ] **C** Because he wanted to get paid as much money as possible
- [ ] **D** Because the lawns were so large
- [ ] **E** Because of bad weather

(9) **What was a ration book for?**

- [ ] **A** To limit the food you could buy to ensure supplies didn't run out
- [ ] **B** To show whose turn it was to go on watch
- [ ] **C** To show you different ways to cook bacon and eggs
- [ ] **D** To list all the different things you could buy in a department store
- [ ] **E** To list all the different things you could buy in Mr Johnson's store

(10) **Which word is closest in meaning to 'barely' as it is used in line 18?**

- [ ] **A** Unhappily
- [ ] **B** Quickly
- [ ] **C** Hardly
- [ ] **D** Fortunately
- [ ] **E** Unfortunately

SPELLING

05:00
5 minutes

In these sentences there are some spelling mistakes.

In each sentence, there is either one spelling mistake or no mistake. Find the group of words with the mistake in it and circle **A, B, C** or **D.**

If there is no mistake, circle **N.**

1. The most dificult thing about the examination was the long essay question at the end.

   A   B   C   D   **N**

2. Anticipating the start as best as she could, Amy sprinted away from the other atheletes.

   A   B   C   D   **N**

3. The undercover police officers had successfully infiltrated the criminal gang at last.

   A   B   C   D   **N**

4. Although we were all acustomed to the tough training schedule, it was still gruelling.

   A   B   C   D   **N**

5. It was only hearsay, but the gossip was that the neighbours had been away all month.

   A   B   C   D   **N**

6. Our challenge was to complete the obstacle course with no hesitation or trepydation.

   A   B   C   D   **N**

7. The conductor was leading the orcestra beautifully, waving his arms rhythmically.

   A   B   C   D   **N**

8. The only lingering doubt we had about the party was weather anyone would attend.

   A   B   C   D   **N**

9. He enjoyed snowboarding so much that he practiced every day when he came home.

   A   B   C   D   **N**

10. Unsurprisingly, the poor forecast meant that the cricket compitition was postponed.

    A   B   C   D   **N**

PUNCTUATION

In these sentences there are some punctuation mistakes.

In each sentence, there is either one punctuation mistake or no mistake. Find the group of words with the mistake in it and circle A, B, C or D.

If there is no mistake, circle N.

1. "Hurry up and come back" said Mohammed, well aware that time was running out.
   A   B   C   D   N

2. There was no doubt that the farmers field was in poor condition after he neglected it.
   A   B   C   D   N

3. "Should I wear a jumper when I go outside or is the weather not as cold as it looks."
   A   B   C   D   N

4. The car was showing it's age by shaking violently when the driver tried to accelerate.
   A   B   C   D   N

5. Most of the gathering, having arrived as early as midday were making plans to leave.
   A   B   C   D   N

6. The ancient book referred to a 'dowry'; Samuel had finally found what he needed.
   A   B   C   D   N

7. Carefully negotiating the potholes in the road the horse and carriage made progress.
   A   B   C   D   N

8. "How many times do we need to let you know, that it's dangerous to play over there?"
   A   B   C   D   N

9. The supermarket, packed with supplies after a fresh delivery, had lots' of bargains.
   A   B   C   D   N

10. "Look at the rainbow!" Exclaimed Ranjeet, who hadn't seen one in real life before.
    A   B   C   D   N

GRAMMAR

05:00
5 minutes

Choose the best word, or group of words, to complete each sentence.

Circle A, B, C, D or E.

1. Soldiers **A) isn't B) was C) wasn't D) weren't E) can't** allowed to fall asleep on duty.

2. It is better to try **A) to B) the C) little D) too E) right** hard than not at all.

3. Optimists always **A) want B) believe C) will D) was E) berate** that something good will happen.

4. Only a fool **A) does B) doesn't C) that D) this E) look** take care when they cross the road.

5. Although the gentleman **A) were B) was C) will be D) is E) isn't** charming, he wasn't to be trusted.

6. The **A) whether B) water C) weather D) sun E) forethought** took a turn for the worse and the rain poured down.

7. The teacher **A) decided B) debated C) discourse D) detoured E) deplored** that Kassim should be a prefect without asking anyone else.

8. The government creates **A) legals B) legal C) legislation D) juries E) laments** that helps run the country.

9. We **A) did B) still C) wood D) does E) would** always be happy to return here.

10. London and Cardiff **A) aren't B) our C) are D) here E) were** the capital cities of England and Wales.

**THIS PAGE HAS DELIBERATELY
BEEN LEFT BLANK**

COMPREHENSION AND SPELLING,

PUNCTUATION & GRAMMAR 2

Look out for Billy's tips and hints.

LEARN: PUNCTUATION

Good punctuation is very important so that the reader can understand the true meaning of what is being written.

Using Commas

- **Lists**

  Commas are used to separate items in a list. For example: She went to the shops and bought grapes, potatoes, a cabbage and ice cream.

  In a list, the final item should be 'and' rather than a comma.

- **Independent clauses**

  Commas are also used to connect two independent clauses, usually with the words 'and', 'but', 'so', 'for', 'not' and 'yet'. For example: I went to the gym, but I forgot my pass.

- **Separating elements**

  Commas help to break up sentences and introductory elements. For example: The car, wheels spinning, raced off the start line.

Example question 1

Put commas in the correct places in this sentence.

The sun having come out from behind the clouds gave off a dazzling glare.

Using End Punctuation

- **Full stops**

  Full stops are used at the end of most sentences. For example: She went to the cinema.

- **Question marks**

  Question marks are used at the end of a sentence if it is a question. For example: What time did she go to the cinema?

- **Exclamation marks**

  Exclamation marks are used when something extraordinary has happened and extra emphasis is needed. They should not be used unnecessarily. For example: The cinema has been evacuated!

Example question 2

Put the correct punctuation at the end of these sentences.

The building is on fire

How many lessons do we have this afternoon

The road is quite long

Using Colons

Colons are used to introduce something or a series of things that adds extra information to whatever came before the colon. For example: Three people went to the cinema: Joyce, Ranjeet and Lucy.

Colons are most commonly used with lists. For example: This is what we will need for the trip: swimming costumes, a packed lunch and our maps.

Example question 3

Put the correct punctuation into this sentence.

There are three types of triangles isosceles, equilateral and scalene.

Using Semi-Colons

Semi-colons are used to join two related independent clauses. They are used instead of a comma and a coordinating conjunction (such as 'and', 'but', 'or'). A semi-colon should only be used if the sentence remains clear to understand without the coordinating conjunction.

For example: The cinema was evacuated; Ranjeet went for a meal instead.

Example question 4

Put the correct punctuation into this sentence.

The car had broken down Joe decided to walk home.

Using Speech Marks

Speech marks, or quotation marks, are used to indicate direct speech or to highlight a quote.

For example: "Let's go to the beach," said Ayesha, hoping we would agree.

Read frequently and you will see how authors use punctuation marks correctly to make their work easy to read and understand.

COMPREHENSION

Read the passage below and then answer the questions that follow.

The Problem of Plastic in our Oceans

1   It is an alarming fact that over 12 million tonnes of plastic are discarded into the world's oceans every year. The main issue with plastic is that it is indestructible. It is quite a thought that every single piece of plastic ever created is still on the planet today.

Plastic in the ocean affects the food chain. Waterborne chemicals – 'toxins' – cling to the
5   discarded plastic. When these plastics mix with plankton, they are eaten by fish and become part of the food chain.

Once ingested by fish, these toxins are released from the plastic fragments, carried in the bloodstream and stored in the fatty tissues of the fish. Humans eat these fish and the toxins enter our bodies. These toxins have been linked with serious diseases in humans.
10   More than two-thirds of the world's fish stock are suffering from plastic ingestion.

The world produces 381 million tonnes in plastic waste every year and that is predicted to double by 2034. Half of this is 'single-use' – the plastic is used once and then discarded. Under 10% is recycled for further use.

It is time for action to fight this issue and there are ways that we can all help. We can reduce
15   our purchasing of single-use plastics, such as plastic bags, water bottles, straws, cups and utensils. There are other items we can buy instead that do not cause such a problem.

We can all try to recycle the plastic that is used. 99% of all UK local authorities now offer collection facilities for plastic bottles, either through household recycling collections or at recycling centres. In addition, more and more local authorities are now offering
20   collections for mixed plastics packaging such as pots, tubs and trays.

A fun thing to do can be to participate in beach clean-up days. Have a look around and try to find one that is happening near you. A group of people comb the beach for plastics and remove them for proper recycling.

Finally, remember that you have a voice and an influence. Read more about the subject;
25   join and follow the organisations that push for a clean-up of the world's oceans. Tell your friends and write to your local MP. Let's make sure as many people know about this issue as possible.

① **Why is all the plastic ever created still on the planet today?**

- [ ] **A** Because there is no desire to destroy it
- [ ] **B** We are not told.
- [ ] **C** Because the ocean protects it
- [ ] **D** Because it is so useful to our everyday lives
- [ ] **E** Because it is impossible to destroy

② **What are the toxins that are described in the passage?**

- [ ] **A** Pieces of contaminated plastic
- [ ] **B** Plankton at the bottom of the food chain
- [ ] **C** Chemicals that live in the water
- [ ] **D** We are not told.
- [ ] **E** Sea water that created plastic

③ **What type of word is 'fatty' as it is used in line 8?**

- [ ] **A** Adjective
- [ ] **B** Noun
- [ ] **C** Verb
- [ ] **D** Adverb
- [ ] **E** Prepositon

④ **How do the toxins end up affecting humans?**

- [ ] **A** Through fishers coming into contact with affected fish
- [ ] **B** When they eat the affected fish
- [ ] **C** Through contaminated fish tanks
- [ ] **D** When the plastic is recycled
- [ ] **E** We are not told.

⑤ **Which of these words is closest in meaning to 'discarded' as it is used in line 13?**

- [ ] **A** Displayed
- [ ] **B** Dismayed
- [ ] **C** Discombobulated
- [ ] **D** Jettisoned
- [ ] **E** Recycled

⑥ **How urgent is the plastic in our oceans issue?**

- [ ] **A** We are not told.
- [ ] **B** Not urgent at all
- [ ] **C** Extremely urgent
- [ ] **D** Reasonably urgent
- [ ] **E** Everything that can be done is already being done.

⑦ **Which of these statements is true about single-use plastics?**

- [ ] **A** They are used because there is no alternative.
- [ ] **B** They are all used once and then discarded into the sea.
- [ ] **C** They are eventually destroyed.
- [ ] **D** There are alternative products that can be used.
- [ ] **E** None of the above statements are true.

⑧ **How are local authorities in the UK helping?**

- [ ] **A** By offering plastic recycling facilities
- [ ] **B** They are not helping at all.
- [ ] **C** We are not told.
- [ ] **D** By cleaning the oceans of plastic
- [ ] **E** By spending money on research

⑨ **How are people recruited to comb beaches for plastics?**

- [ ] **A** By the local authorities
- [ ] **B** They are paid by the big plastic producers.
- [ ] **C** People living in coastal areas are selected at random.
- [ ] **D** By looking for volunteers
- [ ] **E** It is compulsory for people living in coastal areas.

⑩ **Which of these words best describes this passage?**

- [ ] **A** Unfortunate
- [ ] **B** Sarcastic
- [ ] **C** Ironic
- [ ] **D** Farcical
- [ ] **E** Motivational

SPELLING

05:00
5 minutes

In these sentences there are some spelling mistakes.

In each sentence, there is either one spelling mistake or no mistake. Find the group of words with the mistake in it and circle A, B, C or D.

If there is no mistake, circle N.

① *The Lion, the Which and the Wardrobe* continues to remain one of my favourite novels.

  A   B   C   D   N

② He continued on his travells despite the many adversities that he constantly faced.

  A   B   C   D   N

③ She plunged her trustey sword deep into the heart of the mighty and formidable beast.

  A   B   C   D   N

④ *The Lion King* was adapted into a sensational and phenomenally successful stage musicle.

  A   B   C   D   N

⑤ The exhibitor was accussed of both fabrication and exaggeration when relating the tales.

  A   B   C   D   N

⑥ Of coarse, it was extremely fortuitous that the earthquake struck in such a remote area.

  A   B   C   D   N

⑦ A successful assent of the mountain that towered above me was crucial to my mission.

  A   B   C   D   N

⑧ We were astonished by the lack of responsibility that the perpetrators had shown.

  A   B   C   D   N

⑨ The eager students were desperately hopping to unearth the information at the museum.

  A   B   C   D   N

⑩ He told us a story so peculier that we could all scarcely believe his incoherent ramblings.

  A   B   C   D   N

PUNCTUATION

In these sentences there are some punctuation mistakes.

In each sentence, there is either one punctuation mistake or no mistake. Find the group of words with the mistake in it and circle A, B, C or D.

If there is no mistake, circle N.

① Its always an interesting experience to go to a different country and see how others live.

    A   B   C   D   **N**

② I am travelling to visit aunt Julia; she lives in the North of England, close to Scotland.

    A   B   C   D   **N**

③ I think that hunting is a disgraceful way to occupy your time: it's quite barbaric?

    A   B   C   D   **N**

④ Suffice it to say that there's little to choose between being eaten by a lion or a crocodile

    A   B   C   D   **N**

⑤ Disappointingly, both museum's exhibits weren't as impressive as we'd hoped they'd be.

    A   B   C   D   **N**

⑥ We diligently gathered the wood but we had to ask a grown up to light the fire.

    A   B   C   D   **N**

⑦ Since there was no escaping the beast, there was only one thing that we could do: hide.

    A   B   C   D   **N**

⑧ Is economy with the truth different to telling lies. It's not easy to respond succinctly, is it?

    A   B   C   D   **N**

⑨ They visited Mrs Poonam's house first, then made their way to the nearest Bridge.

    A   B   C   D   **N**

⑩ Both hotel's facilities weren't as impressive as we had expected and we were upset.

    A   B   C   D   **N**

GRAMMAR

05:00
5 minutes

Choose the best word, or group of words, to complete each sentence.

Circle A, B, C, D or E.

① I didn't know **A) nothing B) great deal C) lot D) anything E) him** about hunting at that time.

② Lions are the **A) really B) quite C) most D) scariest E) extremely** ferocious of beasts.

③ I have **A) watch B) been watching C) watched D) looked E) liked** the award-winning film lots of times.

④ You go in this **A) way B) weigh C) road D) direction E) time** and I'll go in that direction.

⑤ Despite his seemingly hopeless predicament, he managed to **A) invade B) evade C) evoke D) invoke E) erase** the jaws of both animals.

⑥ I **A) concerned B) resume C) presume D) presumed E) consume** that he is lost: he should have been here by now.

⑦ I **A) couldn't B) could of C) will have D) must have E) should've** known better than to rush my answers.

⑧ "Who put **A) forward B) up C) in D) down E) away** the idea that we should go to the park in the first place?"

⑨ I decided to defend myself with my bow and arrow **A) whereby B) whereas C) wherefore D) wherein E) wherever** my companion chose his legs ... and ran!

⑩ "I **A) did it B) do it C) done it D) does it E) doing it** first", cried the excited child as they fitted the last piece of the puzzle.

**THIS PAGE HAS DELIBERATELY
BEEN LEFT BLANK**

COMPREHENSION AND SPELLING,

PUNCTUATION & GRAMMAR 3

Look out for Billy's tips and hints.

LEARN: SPELLING SKILLS

The best way to improve your spelling is to practise. Read a lot, jot down words that are tricky to spell and you will soon find your spelling improving.

For words that you find particularly tricky, there are some fun ways to improve your spelling, including mnemonics, phonological awareness, common prefixes, common suffixes and spelling rules.

Mnemonics

Mnemonics can be a useful way of helping you to remember how to spell tricky words.

For example, rhythm is a tough word to spell correctly. So create a mnemonic for it that you will find fun and remember, such as: **R**ain **h**as **y**our **t**oes **h**airy **m**aybe.

A mnemonic doesn't need to make sense, or even be logical, it just needs to be something that you personally will be able to remember. You could use friends' names, or whatever you like. That's the fun part – it is personal to you!

Once you remember the mnemonic, then all you do is take the first letter of each word in the same order.

Example question 1

Create your own mnemonic for 'seize'.

Phonological Awareness

Developing your phonological awareness skills is a natural way of improving your spelling. This includes identifying rhyming words, understanding the number of syllables in a word, recognising alliteration and segmenting a sentence into words.

With spelling, phonological awareness means dividing a word into its phonemes as you spell the word. Consider the word 'particular', for example. Read the word aloud and separate out the parts, or syllables. You get *par*, *tic*, *ul* and *ar*. This can give you a general guide to how you spell the word.

Common Prefixes

A prefix is found at the start of a word. Try to learn and understand some of the most common word prefixes, what they mean and how they are spelt.

Prefix	Meaning	Example
fore-	before	foresee
em-	cause to	embrace
sub-	below	substandard
anti-	against	antidote
inter-	between	intertwine

Common Suffixes

A suffix is found at the end of a word. Try to learn and understand some of the most common suffixes, what they mean and how they are spelt.

Suffix	Meaning	Example
-able	can be done	comfortable
-en	made of	wooden
-ful	full of	mournful
-less	without	careless
-ly	characteristic of	dourly

Spelling Rules

Spelling rules can be tricky because there are always exceptions to a rule. However, it can definitely help your spelling if you understand some common spelling rules.

For example: *i* before *e* except after *c*

Generally, in words containing *ie*, the *ie* appears in that order unless it is after *c*.

Example question 2

Give three words where this rule is **true**.

Example question 3

Give three words where this rule is **false**.

Here is another spelling rule: When you add a suffix that starts with *e* (such as -*ed*, -*er* or -*est*) to a word that ends in *y*, the *y* usually changes to an *i*.

Example question 4

Give three examples where this rule is **true**.

Example question 5

Give one example where this rule is **false**.

Remember, these spelling rules are not always correct – but they are a useful guide. Nothing can replace reading widely and practising spelling words.

COMPREHENSION

15:00
15 minutes

Read the passage below and then answer the questions that follow.

Boudicca

1 "Those who do not learn history are doomed to repeat it." This quote is most likely owed to writer and philosopher George Santana. The idea that history repeats itself is hard to disagree with. History offers us stories about great men and women who inspire us to embrace hope, courage and humility. Learning about their lives is important because it

5 allows us to understand the past, which in turn helps us to comprehend our present and improve our future. Who then was Boudicca, and what can we learn from her life?

Boudicca was the legendary chief of the Iceni tribe who ruled East Anglia two thousand years ago. She inherited the title from her husband when he died, in accordance with the laws of her tribe. Unfortunately, this conflicted with the practice of the Romans (who

10 had invaded Britain in 43 CE) whose laws allowed inheritance only through the male line. Consequently, they not only took her kingdom, but also publicly flogged her and ill-treated her daughters. Because Boudicca came from an aristocratic family, she had been trained to fight. Boudicca refused to be so disrespected and was incited to rebellion and revenge. She would undoubtedly have agreed with Calamity Jane who said, "… If a

15 girl wants to be a legend, she should go ahead and be one."

Using her wealth and intelligence, Boudicca led an uprising of all the Celtic tribes against the mighty power of the occupying Roman forces. She must have been an inspiring warrior: with her tall, striking appearance and flaming red hair she led her warriors bravely into battle against a foe that was better trained and equipped, and far exceeded

20 her soldiers in numbers. Her bravery came from her cause. "We British are used to women commanders in war… I am fighting as an ordinary person for my lost freedom, my bruised body, and my outraged daughters. That is what I, a woman, plan to do! Let the men live in slavery if they will," was her battle cry.

Boudicca was initially triumphant. She ransacked and destroyed the key settlements of

25 Colchester, St Albans and London, burning them to the ground and slaughtering their citizens. She left her mark, literally: if you dig deep enough below the ground upon which these cities sat you will find a thick layer of red soot even today. Boudicca and her army were finally defeated in The Battle of Watling Street where an inferior quality of weaponry (despite outnumbering the opposing forces) assured the Celtic downfall. Many of her men ran

30 away in the face of the overwhelming might of the Roman forces and many of those captured were made slaves. No one knows what happened to Boudicca, although it is claimed in some sources that she committed suicide rather than face the ignominy of capture.

What then can we learn from Boudicca's story? Whether she was a heroine or villain I will leave you to decide for yourself. However, we can all surely learn from her resolute refusal

35 to bow meekly to injustice. She is a symbol of encouragement to those of us (boy or girl) who struggle to be assertive, and feel pressure to be conciliatory and likeable at all times. Next time someone tries to steal your thunder, refuse to be side-lined. Defend ideas that are yours resolutely… although probably best not to use the weaponry and arson!

1. **What type of word is 'humility' (line 4)?**
   - ☐ **A** A common noun
   - ☐ **B** An adjective
   - ☐ **C** A proper noun
   - ☐ **D** A collective noun
   - ☐ **E** An abstract noun

2. **'Her bravery came from her cause.' (line 20)**
   What does this mean?
   - ☐ **A** Boudicca was inspired by other people.
   - ☐ **B** Boudicca was brave because she was a woman.
   - ☐ **C** Boudicca's beliefs made her brave.
   - ☐ **D** Boudicca caused a lot of trouble.
   - ☐ **E** There was cause for concern about Boudicca's bravery.

3. **What does the text tell us about the importance of studying history?**
   - ☐ **A** It will give us courage.
   - ☐ **B** We will enjoy the exciting stories.
   - ☐ **C** We will agree with what people did.
   - ☐ **D** It will help us to understand why the world is like it is today.
   - ☐ **E** We will not make the same mistakes again.

4. **Which of the following is a good idiom to describe the desire to be 'conciliatory' (line 36)?**
   - ☐ **A** To let the cat out of the bag
   - ☐ **B** To get your act together
   - ☐ **C** To give it a shot
   - ☐ **D** To pour oil on troubled waters
   - ☐ **E** To pass with flying colours

5. **Which word best describes how Boudicca reacted to the actions of the Romans following the death of her husband?**
   - ☐ **A** Outsmarted
   - ☐ **B** Infuriated
   - ☐ **C** Upset
   - ☐ **D** Resigned
   - ☐ **E** Jovial

6. **What does the writer of the passage say about the example that Boudicca's story sets for us today?**
   - ☐ **A** The writer leaves the reader to make up their own mind.
   - ☐ **B** We should stick up for ourselves.
   - ☐ **C** We should learn to be submissive.
   - ☐ **D** Rules are made to be broken.
   - ☐ **E** Girls are always right.

⑦ **Under the laws of the Roman Empire, who were titles and land passed on to after death?**

☐ **A** Daughters
☐ **B** Wives
☐ **C** Sons
☐ **D** Best friends
☐ **E** Any family member

⑧ **Why did Boudicca's forces lose The Battle of Watling Street?**

☐ **A** They had too few soldiers.
☐ **B** They didn't have enough guns.
☐ **C** The soldiers were scared and all ran away.
☐ **D** The Romans had better weapons.
☐ **E** Boudicca's tactics were poor.

⑨ **In the context of this text, what does 'legend' (line 15) mean?**

☐ **A** A traditional historic story
☐ **B** A caption
☐ **C** An inscription on a Roman medal
☐ **D** A story about a saint
☐ **E** An extremely famous person

⑩ **Why might you find a thick layer of red sediment if you dig deep into the ground below Colchester?**

☐ **A** Boudicca had red hair.
☐ **B** It is stained with the blood of people slaughtered there a long time ago.
☐ **C** The soil has a lot of iron in it.
☐ **D** It is evidence that Colchester was destroyed by fire in Roman times.
☐ **E** Historians are unable to explain this phenomenon.

SPELLING

05:00
5 minutes

In these sentences there are some spelling mistakes.

In each sentence, there is either one spelling mistake or no mistake. Find the group of words with the mistake in it and circle **A, B, C** or **D**.

If there is no mistake, circle **N**.

1. The Romans ransacked Boudicca's territories and possessions, and had her whiped.
   A　　　B　　　C　　　D　　　N

2. Historical accounts attest that Boudicca was strikeing, with fierce eyes and auburn hair.
   A　　　B　　　C　　　D　　　N

3. From Boudicca we are inspired to endevour to be brave and courageous in adversity.
   A　　　B　　　C　　　D　　　N

4. Famous rebellions and uprisings often give rise to unforgettable heros and heroines.
   A　　　B　　　C　　　D　　　N

5. Gandhi's whole career was won brilliant, non-violent uprising called civil disobedience.
   A　　　B　　　C　　　D　　　N

6. Women who fought to be recognised as equal in the passed are now admired greatly.
   A　　　B　　　C　　　D　　　N

7. Elizabeth I reigned for longer and more successfully than any other Tudor monarch.
   A　　　B　　　C　　　D　　　N

8. Malala Yousafzai was 16 when she publicly spoke out on woman's rights to education.
   A　　　B　　　C　　　D　　　N

9. Amelia Earhart, an aviator, was the definition of a rule braker and a trailblazer.
   A　　　B　　　C　　　D　　　N

10. Anne Frank's tragic story has touched the soles of many and is remembered globally.
    A　　　B　　　C　　　D　　　N

PUNCTUATION

05:00
5 minutes

In these sentences there are some punctuation mistakes.

In each sentence, there is either one punctuation mistake or no mistake. Find the group of words with the mistake in it and circle A, B, C or D.

If there is no mistake, circle N.

1. they decided to visit the beach as soon as the weather was nice enough.

   A   B   C   D   **N**

2. How many items of clothing should we pack before going on our trip.

   A   B   C   D   **N**

3. The car was brand new so the owner was driving it as carefully as she could

   A   B   C   D   **N**

4. The group of friends, was walking down the street looking for a taxi.

   A   B   C   D   **N**

5. The plane had been damaged on the previous flight and it's crew were fixing it.

   A   B   C   D   **N**

6. She went to the supermarket and bought carrots, potatoes, drinks, and crisps.

   A   B   C   D   **N**

7. "The tide comes in very quickly," Pointed out Caleb, who was a keen surfer.

   A   B   C   D   **N**

8. The teachers' classroom had been left in a mess and he was very cross.

   A   B   C   D   **N**

9. Most Saturdays, my father goes to the shops to get something nice for dinner!

   A   B   C   D   **N**

10. The walls' of the building were showing signs of wear, as were the carpets.

    A   B   C   D   **N**

GRAMMAR

05:00
5 minutes

Choose the best word, or group of words, to complete each sentence.

Circle A, B, C, D or E.

1. They planned to launch a surprise attack **A) into B) at C) under D) around E) when** the cover of darkness.

2. It **A) must of B) can have C) was D) must have E) certainly was** been devastating to see your city and home completely ransacked.

3. Nowadays it is **A) accepting B) accepted C) acceptance D) in acceptance E) acceptably** that women should be able to fight on the frontline.

4. While there are still more women than men in nursing, the number of men **A) are B) might C) slowly D) must E) is** increasing.

5. You should not allow your choice of career to be **A) determined B) determination C) detoured D) deterrent E) determinedly** by your gender identity.

6. The friends had agreed to meet in the high street, but some of **A) she B) that C) him D) he E) them** forgot that.

7. History is my favourite subject to study **A) because B) although C) regardless D) sometimes E) despite** I dislike having to write commentaries about events.

8. I **A) to B) two C) too D) so E) totally** am excited by the prospect of tackling a new subject.

9. Having read about her, I am **A) keening B) eagerly C) welcome D) keen E) enthusing** to learn more about who Calamity Jane was.

10. We all hoped **A) their B) two C) that D) they E) time** our homework deadline would be extended.

THIS PAGE HAS DELIBERATELY BEEN LEFT BLANK

COMPREHENSION AND SPELLING, PUNCTUATION & GRAMMAR 4

Look out for Billy's tips and hints.

LEARN: LITERARY DEVICES

Most comprehension tests will have a question on literary devices. You will usually be asked to identify what type of literary device is being used, or to find an example of a certain literary device that is being used in the text.

In the comprehension test on pages 40–42, Question 6 is a literary device question.

Let's look at the main types of literacy device.

Simile

A simile is used by writers to make a description more vivid to the reader. It offers a comparison between one thing and another. For example: The child ran as fast as a whippet. You can often identify a simile because it uses a comparison word such as 'like' or 'as'.

Example question 1

Identify the simile in this sentence.

Although he was often nervous before a big show, on this occasion his veins were as cold as ice. He didn't feel a thing.

Metaphor

It is easy to get confused between a simile and a metaphor. This is because a metaphor is also comparing two things for effect. However, a metaphor compares two things that, although similar, cannot be a statement that is actually true. So a metaphor does not use 'like' or 'as'.

For example, if your brother likes to get up early, a metaphor might be: Sid is an early bird. Like a bird, he gets up early, but he is not actually a bird. The simile would be: Sid gets up as early as a bird.

Example question 2

Identify the metaphor in this sentence.

We had received so much homework that I was absolutely drowning in it.

You may get asked why an author has used a particular literary device at certain points of a text. Understand why they are used!

Alliteration

Alliteration is when a writer uses the same sound at the beginning of words that are close to each other. It has the effect of making the passage more fun and engaging to read. An example of alliteration is: The snake slithered along the slippery slope.

Remember, not many of the words need to have the same sound, it could just be two. Also, don't make the mistake of just looking for the same letter; it is the same sound that matters. 'He is pleased with the phonetics of his writing' is not an example of alliteration – although 'pleased' and 'phonetics' both start with the letter 'p', they do not sound the same when spoken.

Example question 3

Identify the alliteration in these sentences.

The forest came to life at night. Nocturnal animals went about their business. Squirrels searched for supplies. Deer looked as calm as the stillest river as they strolled about.

Onomatopoeia

Onomatopoeia is when words that are said out loud sound exactly like what they are describing. For example, 'boom' and 'beep' are examples of onomatopoeia. If you say the words out loud, they imitate the sound they are describing.

Example question 4

Identify the two examples of onomatopoeia in these sentences.

The prison warder patrolled the corridors watchfully. Her shoes squeaked as she moved along the floor. Suddenly she heard a loud bang from one of the cells.

Idiom

An idiom is an expression, word or phrase that should not be taken literally. It is usually a well-known collection of words that does not actually mean what the words say. For example, a common phrase is: It is raining cats and dogs. People know that this means it is raining heavily and not that it is actually raining cats and dogs!

Example question 5

Identify the idiom that is used in these sentences.

Krishan felt guilty. He didn't want to be the one who spilled the beans, but he felt like he was given no choice. If he hadn't revealed all, then people could have got hurt.

Learn the literary devices and what they do. Look out for them in passages!

COMPREHENSION

Read the passage below and then answer the questions that follow.

The Golden Touch (by Nathaniel Hawthorne)

King Midas is visited by a stranger with supernatural powers who grants him a wish.

1   Midas was enjoying himself in his treasure-room, one day, as usual, when he perceived a shadow fall over the heaps of gold; and, looking suddenly up, what should he behold but the figure of a stranger, standing in the bright and narrow sunbeam! It was a young man, with a cheerful and ruddy face. Whether it was that the imagination of King Midas threw
5   a yellow tinge over everything, or whatever the cause might be, he could not help fancying that the smile with which the stranger regarded him had a kind of golden radiance in it. Certainly, although his figure intercepted the sunshine, there was now a brighter gleam upon all the piled-up treasures than before. Even the remotest corners had their share of it, and were lighted up, when the stranger smiled, as with tips of flame
10 and sparkles of fire.

As Midas knew that he had carefully turned the key in the lock, and that no mortal strength could possibly break into his treasure-room, he, of course, concluded that his visitor must be something more than mortal. It is no matter about telling you who he was. In those days, when the earth was comparatively a new affair, it was supposed to
15 be often the resort of beings endowed with supernatural power, and who used to interest themselves in the joys and sorrows of men, women, and children, half playfully and half seriously.

Midas had met such beings before now, and was not sorry to meet one of them again. The stranger's aspect, indeed, was so good-humoured and kindly, if not beneficent, that
20 it would have been unreasonable to suspect him of intending any mischief. It was far more probable that he came to do Midas a favour. And what could that favour be, unless to multiply his heaps of treasure?

The stranger gazed about the room; and when his lustrous smile had glistened upon all the golden objects that were there, he turned again to Midas.

25 "You are a wealthy man, friend Midas!" he observed. "I doubt whether any other four walls, on earth, contain so much gold as you have contrived to pile up in this room."

"I have done pretty well,—pretty well," answered Midas, in a discontented tone. "But, after all, it is but a trifle, when you consider that it has taken me my whole life to get it together. If one could live a thousand years, he might have time to grow rich!"

30 "What!" exclaimed the stranger. "Then you are not satisfied?"

Midas shook his head.

"And pray what would satisfy you?" asked the stranger. "Merely for the curiosity of the thing, I should be glad to know."

35 Midas paused and meditated. He felt a presentiment that this stranger, with such a golden lustre in his good-humoured smile, had come hither with both the power and the purpose of gratifying his utmost wishes. Now, therefore, was the fortunate moment, when he had but to speak, and obtain whatever possible, or seemingly impossible thing, it might come into his head to ask. So he thought, and thought, and thought, and heaped up one golden mountain upon another, in his imagination, without being able to imagine
40 them big enough. At last, a bright idea occurred to King Midas. It seemed really as bright as the glistening metal which he loved so much.

Raising his head, he looked the lustrous stranger in the face.

"Well, Midas," observed his visitor, "I see that you have at length hit upon something that will satisfy you. Tell me your wish."

45 "It is only this," replied Midas. "I am weary of collecting my treasures with so much trouble, and beholding the heap so diminutive, after I have done my best. I wish everything that I touch to be changed to gold!"

① **Why was King Midas enjoying himself at the beginning of the passage?**
- [ ] **A** He was pleased the young man had arrived.
- [ ] **B** He liked the sunbeams coming through the window.
- [ ] **C** He loved spending time with his treasure.
- [ ] **D** He was relieved that the door was locked.
- [ ] **E** He was pleased that his piles of gold were growing.

② **What did King Midas imagine when the young visitor smiled?**
- [ ] **A** That sunbeams came into the treasure room.
- [ ] **B** That his piles of gold grew bigger.
- [ ] **C** That the fire started to sparkle.
- [ ] **D** That a shadow fell across the room.
- [ ] **E** That the gold gleamed even more brightly.

③ **What is a synonym for 'perceived' (line 1)?**
- [ ] **A** Saw
- [ ] **B** Mistook
- [ ] **C** Moved
- [ ] **D** Felt
- [ ] **E** Received

④ **How did King Midas know that the visitor was no ordinary mortal?**
- [ ] **A** The visitor had a ruddy complexion.
- [ ] **B** The visitor was extraordinarily beautiful.
- [ ] **C** No one could have known about his treasure.
- [ ] **D** The door was locked and a human couldn't have got in.
- [ ] **E** The young man came in through the window.

⑤ **What part of speech is the word 'discontented' (line 27)?**
- ☐ **A** Adjective
- ☐ **B** Noun
- ☐ **C** Adverb
- ☐ **D** Article
- ☐ **E** Pronoun

⑥ **King Midas's idea is described 'as bright as the glistening metal which he loved so much' (lines 40–41). What is this an example of?**
- ☐ **A** Irony
- ☐ **B** Metaphor
- ☐ **C** Simile
- ☐ **D** Personification
- ☐ **E** Indirect speech

⑦ **In line 30, the visitor exclaims to King Midas: "What! Then you are not satisfied?" Why is King Midas not satisfied?**
- ☐ **A** He has all the treasure he needs.
- ☐ **B** He wants every wish to come true.
- ☐ **C** He has no one to share his treasure with.
- ☐ **D** He believes that it has taken too long to amass his treasure.
- ☐ **E** He would like to be young and beautiful again.

⑧ **What is an antonym of the word 'diminutive' (line 46)?**
- ☐ **A** Small
- ☐ **B** Minuscule
- ☐ **C** Lengthening
- ☐ **D** Enormous
- ☐ **E** Dreary

⑨ **What type of story do you think this is?**
- ☐ **A** A report
- ☐ **B** A myth
- ☐ **C** An account
- ☐ **D** A historical novel
- ☐ **E** Science fiction

⑩ **Based on what you know from the passage, how is the story likely to end?**
- ☐ **A** King Midas will realise that the young visitor has come to trick him.
- ☐ **B** The young man will persuade King Midas to give up his treasure.
- ☐ **C** King Midas will be granted his wish, which will have disastrous consequences.
- ☐ **D** King Midas will lose all his treasure.
- ☐ **E** The young man will turn into gold.

SPELLING

05:00
5 minutes

In these sentences there are some spelling mistakes.

In each sentence, there is either one spelling mistake or no mistake. Find the group of words with the mistake in it and circle A, B, C or D.

If there is no mistake, circle N.

1. King Midas thoroughly enjoyed spending time in his tresure-room.
   A   B   C   D   N

2. The prechious metal gold shines with the brightness of warmest sunbeams.
   A   B   C   D   N

3. Humans are mortal creetures and are not bestowed with supernatural powers.
   A   B   C   D   N

4. People have commented on many occassions that money is the root of all evil.
   A   B   C   D   N

5. 'Be carefull what you wish for' is an old and very wise adage.
   A   B   C   D   N

6. It can seem impossibly difficult to gain access into a locked room.
   A   B   C   D   N

7. In previous times, when the world was young, supernatural beings were said to be visable.
   A   B   C   D   N

8. King Midas was unfortunate enough to have been bestowed with a very gready soul.
   A   B   C   D   N

9. Throughout history, gold and silver have been prised for their great value.
   A   B   C   D   N

10. Gods used to interest themselves in the joys and sorrows of men, women and children.
    A   B   C   D   N

PUNCTUATION

05:00
5 minutes

In these sentences there are some punctuation mistakes.

In each sentence, there is either one punctuation mistake or no mistake. Find the group of words with the mistake in it and circle A, B, C or D.

If there is no mistake, circle N.

① The golden-haired stranger looked at King Midas and asked, "are you not satisfied?"

     A   B   C   D   N

② Every king is blessed with riches such as gold and jewel's in abundance.

     A   B   C   D   N

③ "How did you get into my treasure chamber?" Asked King Midas as the man appeared.

     A   B   C   D   N

④ Ancient Greek myths are often set upon islands such as Minos, Crete, Lesbos, and Rhodes.

     A   B   C   D   N

⑤ Midas had met similar people before and knew exactly how to handle the situation.

     A   B   C   D   N

⑥ Before answering the young man. King Midas thought about his reply.

     A   B   C   D   N

⑦ The Greek islands are situated towards the East of the Mediterranean Sea.

     A   B   C   D   N

⑧ I stood on a rock my heart was beating fast) and dived into Aegean waters.

     A   B   C   D   N

⑨ Many tiny creatures live in the colourful world beneath the oceans depths.

     A   B   C   D   N

⑩ The treasure had been lit up by the shards of light flooding into the chamber.

     A   B   C   D   N

GRAMMAR

05:00
5 minutes

Choose the best word, or group of words, to complete each sentence.

Circle A, B, C, D or E.

(1) Everyone was **A) detracted B) debated C) distracted D) dispelled E) disaster** by the fireworks.

(2) Twenty minutes **A) passed B) paste C) pass D) past E) pest** midnight is very early in the morning.

(3) She built a **A) comprising B) impelled C) suit D) hope E) compelling** case for why she should be picked.

(4) They **A) shall B) should C) stay D) slow E) shell** have realised that the storm would be dangerous to boats.

(5) The Romans were **A) askew B) institute C) flute D) blended E) astute** at building roads.

(6) She missed his birthday so offered **A) belated B) ballistic C) ballet D) balletic E) bullish** congratulations.

(7) I got **A) margarine B) tangerine C) margin D) partial E) marginally** better results than my sibling.

(8) The spirit is **A) wilful B) willing C) skilful D) careful E) wasn't** but the flesh is weak.

(9) Which **A) whey B) way C) would D) wait E) charm** is fastest to get to the city?

(10) We had a four-hour **A) wind B) height C) clan D) weight E) wait** before we were able to get tickets.

**THIS PAGE HAS DELIBERATELY
BEEN LEFT BLANK**

COMPREHENSION AND SPELLING,

PUNCTUATION & GRAMMAR 5

Look out for Billy's tips and hints.

LEARN: GRAMMAR

Grammar is the way that we arrange words and write sentences so that they make the most sense.

Let's have a look at the key aspects of grammar that you need to know.

Verbs

Verbs are 'doing' words that describe action. For example: I *caught* the ball.

Example question 1

Choose the correct form of the verb.

The children were .... in the playground.

run   ran   running   runs

Adjectives

Adjectives are 'describing' words. They describe a noun. For example: There were *fluffy* clouds high in the sky.

Example question 2

Which word in this sentence is an adjective?

The tall boy crossed the road.

Adverbs

Adverbs further describe verbs, adjectives or even another adverb. They most commonly end in *-ly*, but not always. For example: We *calmly* approached the front gate.

Remember that not all words that end in *-ly* are adverbs.

Example question 3

Which word in this sentence is an adverb?

The herd was slowly moving towards the water hole.

Conjunctions

Conjunctions are words that link parts of a sentence together, such as 'and', 'or', 'but'. For example: Should I go to school *or* stay at home?

Example question 4

Which word in this sentence is a conjunction?

You don't need to go unless you want to.

Prepositions

A preposition is a word that is used before a noun, pronoun or phrase, and shows position, time, place, direction, and so on. For example: We hid *under* the table.

Example question 5

Which of the words in this sentence is a preposition?

She put her homework onto the table.

Pronouns

A pronoun is a word that substitutes a noun, such as 'they', 'it', 'me', 'we', and so on. For example: The friends sat down because *they* were very tired after their trek.

Example question 6

Which of the words in this sentence is a pronoun?

Our teacher was yet to see the best of us.

Nouns

- ### Proper nouns

  A proper noun is a specific name for a place or person. It always starts with a capital letter, wherever the proper noun sits in the sentence. For example: The capital city of *France* is *Paris*.

  ### Example question 7

  Which word in this sentence is a proper noun?

  I turned to my friend Jamie for support.

- ### Concrete nouns

  A concrete noun describes something that is physically real and that you can touch. For example: We entered the *building*.

  Look out for different aspects of grammar as you read!

  ### Example question 8

  Which word in this sentence is a concrete noun?

  We ran quickly over the long grass.

- ### Abstract nouns

  An abstract noun describes an idea, concept or quality. You cannot physically touch it. For example: We go to school to get an *education*.

  ### Example question 9

  Which word in this sentence is an abstract noun?

  Kaveeta used her imagination when writing the story.

COMPREHENSION

Read the passage below and then answer the questions that follow.

A Technical Marvel

1   My grandmother, Evelyn, is exactly six times my age. As a twelve-year-old, I have grown up with technology. "Emma," Gran is fond of saying, "you will get square eyes if you look at that screen for much longer!". I am never really sure what that means, but Mum says that when she was younger Gran would say the same thing to her about watching
5   television.

  Gran was not best pleased when we bought her a smartphone for her birthday. "I will never have a need for this thing!" she barked. Mum was cross with her for being ungrateful, but also for her steadfast refusal to move into the modern era.

  "Mum, these phones are not just for frivolous entertainment! They mean we can keep in
10   touch with you and you can just send quick messages rather than have a long conversation."

  "I like talking. Conversation is a dying art these days. Tap tap tap – that is all I ever see people doing when I walk down the shops! In my day people would stop and have a chat to each other. Now they just bump into you because they are obsessed with their phones," Gran wasn't convinced.

15   A few weeks passed and I went to visit Gran at her house. Strangely, no-one answered the door when I rang the bell. Gran was always in on Thursday afternoons. I tried again and again, and peered through the letterbox. There was no sign of movement. I took out my phone to text Gran and ask where she was. After a few minutes came the reply: "Stuck in garden, patio door won't open. Send help!".

20   A couple of quick phone messages later, my parents came round with their spare keys and released the patio door with a quick shove. It had warped in the rain and got stuck fast when Gran had gone out to water her flowers! There was no path to the front of the house so she was stuck.

  "Why didn't you just text us that you needed help?" said Mum.

25   "I had completely forgotten I had that phone, right until I heard the beep from Emma's text. I wondered what it was – it quite made me jump – but then I suppose it was useful after all!".

  Mum shook her head and Dad gave her a knowing look. I hugged Gran, just relieved that nothing bad had happened to her. "Oh Emma, I promise to think again about
30   technology," said Gran. "I can see it can have its uses!".

① **How old is Evelyn?**
   - ☐ **A**   12
   - ☐ **B**   We are not told.
   - ☐ **C**   60
   - ☐ **D**   82
   - ☐ **E**   72

② **What type of screen did Emma's grandmother think would give her square eyes?**
   - ☐ **A**   A tablet
   - ☐ **B**   A television
   - ☐ **C**   A computer
   - ☐ **D**   We are not told.
   - ☐ **E**   A games console

③ **Which word is most similar in meaning to 'steadfast' as it is used in line 8?**
   - ☐ **A**   Steady
   - ☐ **B**   Quick
   - ☐ **C**   Resolute
   - ☐ **D**   Embarrassing
   - ☐ **E**   Odd

④ **In the second paragraph, what were the two reasons that Emma's mother was cross?**
   - ☐ **A**   Her mother's lack of appreciation and that she wouldn't read the instructions for her new phone.
   - ☐ **B**   Her mother's poor parenting and for not embracing modern technology.
   - ☐ **C**   Her mother's lack of appreciation and for not embracing modern technology.
   - ☐ **D**   Her mother's pessimistic outlook and not thinking of her grandchildren.
   - ☐ **E**   We are not told.

⑤ **What literary device is being used in line 11?**
   - ☐ **A**   Idiom
   - ☐ **B**   Onomatopoeia
   - ☐ **C**   Simile
   - ☐ **D**   Metaphor
   - ☐ **E**   Irony

⑥ **Why would people bump into each other in the street?**
   - ☐ **A**   In the rush to get the latest smartphone
   - ☐ **B**   It is impossible to tell.
   - ☐ **C**   Because they were concentrating on their phones rather than looking at where they were going
   - ☐ **D**   Because they were listening to music
   - ☐ **E**   Because all the screen time made them grumpy

⑦ **Why wouldn't Evelyn's patio door open?**
- ☐ **A** The rain had flooded it.
- ☐ **B** It was locked and she hadn't got the keys with her.
- ☐ **C** It was off its hinges.
- ☐ **D** The rain had caused it to change shape.
- ☐ **E** We are not told.

⑧ **What type of word is 'out' as it is used in line 22?**
- ☐ **A** Noun
- ☐ **B** Verb
- ☐ **C** Preposition
- ☐ **D** Adjective
- ☐ **E** Adverb

⑨ **"Dad gave her a knowing look" (line 28). What is this conveying?**
- ☐ **A** That Emma's parents were surprised that Gran had forgotten about her phone
- ☐ **B** That Emma's dad knew where the phone was all along
- ☐ **C** It is impossible to tell.
- ☐ **D** That now Emma's parents had arrived, they knew all would be fine
- ☐ **E** That Emma's parents were not at all surprised by Gran forgetting about her phone

⑩ **Which of these statements about the passage is true?**
- ☐ **A** The narrator is not part of the story.
- ☐ **B** It is written in the third person.
- ☐ **C** It has a hidden rhyming scheme.
- ☐ **D** It is written in the first person.
- ☐ **E** None of the above statements are true.

SPELLING

05:00
5 minutes

In these sentences there are some spelling mistakes.

In each sentence, there is either one spelling mistake or no mistake. Find the group of words with the mistake in it and circle A, B, C or D.

If there is no mistake, circle N.

① We were devestated to learn that our school team had not qualified for the final.

    A   B   C   D   N

② The worker's computer screen was glowering brightly in the corner of the dark office.

    A   B   C   D   N

③ The manager of the bisness was excited by the new opportunities in the market.

    A   B   C   D   N

④ She claimed to be really enthusiastick about the lesson, but I don't think she was.

    A   B   C   D   N

⑤ Every student at the university knew that the proffessor was the best in her field.

    A   B   C   D   N

⑥ The thieves eventually conffessed to their crime and faced the consequences.

    A   B   C   D   N

⑦ It seemed ridiculous that so few of the class were able to go on the expidition.

    A   B   C   D   N

⑧ We were disapointed to find out that our family home was in need of repair.

    A   B   C   D   N

⑨ The mechanic was quickly able to estimate the value of the vintage vehicle.

    A   B   C   D   N

⑩ I was suprised at how easily I was able to get the top off the ancient bottle.

    A   B   C   D   N

PUNCTUATION

05:00
5 minutes

In these sentences there are some punctuation mistakes.

In each sentence, there is either one punctuation mistake or no mistake. Find the group of words with the mistake in it and circle A, B, C or D.

If there is no mistake, circle N.

1. "What time do we want to go to the park" said Kam, hoping to go early.
   A   B   C   D   N

2. "What should we do if we arrive at the restaurant and it is fully booked."
   A   B   C   D   N

3. The mouse, running away from the cat as fast as it could was looking for cover.
   A   B   C   D   N

4. Mrs Johnsons family home was the biggest in the street and she was a lovely lady.
   A   B   C   D   N

5. The footballer's got on the coach in order to travel home after the crucial match.
   A   B   C   D   N

6. The weather was significantly better than the forecast had predicted it would be.
   A   B   C   D   N

7. London, Cardiff, Edinburgh and Paris are all capital cities; that I have visited.
   A   B   C   D   N

8. The park was shut for the day; we decided to play football in the garden instead.
   A   B   C   D   N

9. She thought it was funny, that her friend had never heard of the famous person.
   A   B   C   D   N

10. The hotel staff, under pressure from their manager were starting to feel the strain.
    A   B   C   D   N

GRAMMAR

 05:00
5 minutes

Choose the best word, or group of words, to complete each sentence.

Circle A, B, C, D or E.

1. The House of Commons **A) isn't B) was C) wasn't D) is E) aren't** where MPs debate motions.

2. The gardener **A) have B) has C) calm D) is E) will** mown the lawn.

3. The puppies **A) are B) our C) vast D) dog E) would** increase the happiness in the house.

4. We **A) go B) run C) went D) walk E) drive** to the beach to sunbathe last weekend.

5. I can see a builder **A) tying B) trying C) list D) tools E) tool** to fix a wall.

6. The sun **A) came B) come C) comes D) could E) can** out and warmed us all up.

7. Our exam is tomorrow **A) some B) so C) shall D) can E) will** we have gone home to revise.

8. An attempted repair of the car **A) proof B) prevent C) prevented D) result E) proved** unfruitful.

9. We are **A) get B) catch C) catching D) caught E) board** a train tomorrow.

10. I am unhappy **A) cause B) chat C) because D) here E) by** my friends forgot about me.

**THIS PAGE HAS DELIBERATELY
BEEN LEFT BLANK**

COMPREHENSION AND SPELLING,

PUNCTUATION & GRAMMAR 6

Look out for Billy's tips and hints.

LEARN: RETRIEVAL AND INFERENCE COMPREHENSION QUESTIONS

There are two main types of question that you will need to answer in order to complete comprehension tasks: retrieval questions and inference questions.

Retrieval Questions

Typically, a retrieval question will ask you something about the passage. The answer will be stated in the passage, so you just have to 'retrieve' the information. Some of these questions will be easy, but some can be tricky, so tread carefully.

For example: *Sami, 68 years old, was the captain of the seniors' football team.*

A straightforward retrieval question would be: *How old was Sami?*

We can see that he is **68** years old.

A slightly trickier retrieval question would be: *What sport did Sami play?*

The answer is football, but you have to read carefully to see this. The text does not say 'Sami plays football', as you might initially expect.

Now read this passage from *Anne of Green Gables* by LM Montgomery, and answer the questions that follow.

For reasons best known to herself, Marilla did not tell Anne that she was to stay at Green Gables until the next afternoon. During the forenoon she kept the child busy with various tasks and watched over her with a keen eye while she did them. By noon she had concluded that Anne was smart and obedient, willing to work and quick to learn; her most serious shortcoming seemed to be a tendency to fall into daydreams in the middle of a task and forget all about it until such time as she was sharply recalled to earth by a reprimand or a catastrophe.

Example question 1

Why did Marilla not tell Anne that she was to stay at Green Gables?

A She was too scared to do so.

B She didn't want to.

C She thought it would scare Anne.

D She didn't want Anne to get over-excited.

E We are not told.

Example question 2

In what way did Marilla watch Anne as she did her tasks?

A Keenly

B Briefly

C Harshly

D Absent-mindedly

E We are not told.

Example question 3

By what time did Marilla come to her judgement on Anne?

A Midnight

B 9 am

C Midday

D The middle of the afternoon

E We are not told.

Remember, not all retrieval questions are straightforward. Always read the text carefully.

Inference Questions

Inference questions are more challenging than retrieval questions because the answer is not explicitly laid out in the text.

You need to read the passage so that you completely understand it. Only then will you be able to answer an inference question. You won't be able to just copy the answer from the passage.

For example: *Sami had finally begun to show his age on the football field. He was certainly not as quick as he used to be.*

An inference question might be: *Why was Sami 'not as quick as he used to be'?*

The answer is: Because he is getting old. We can infer this from 'finally begun to show his age'.

The key to inference questions is to fully understand the text. Read it at least twice.

Now read this passage from *Anne of Green Gables* by LM Montgomery, and answer the questions that follow.

Marilla said nothing to Matthew about the affair that evening; but when Anne proved still refractory the next morning an explanation had to be made to account for her absence from the breakfast table. Marilla told Matthew the whole story, taking pains to impress him with a due sense of the enormity of Anne's behaviour.

"It's a good thing Rachel Lynde got a calling down; she's a meddlesome old gossip," was Matthew's consolatory rejoinder.

"Matthew Cuthbert, I'm astonished at you. You know that Anne's behaviour was dreadful, and yet you take her part! I suppose you'll be saying next thing that she oughtn't to be punished at all."

"Well now—no—not exactly," said Matthew uneasily. "I reckon she ought to be punished a little. But don't be too hard on her, Marilla. Recollect she hasn't ever had anyone to teach her right. You're—you're going to give her something to eat, aren't you?"

Example question 4

What were Marilla's feelings about Anne's behaviour?

A She described it as poor behaviour because she did not like her.

B She described it as poor behaviour and she felt that Anne should be chastised.

C She excused her behaviour because Anne has never been shown good moral qualities.

D She excused her behaviour because she thought it was gossip.

E She described it as poor behaviour and she felt sorry for the other person involved.

Example question 5

How did Matthew's approach to bringing up Anne differ to Marilla's?

A He was more lenient and understanding because of Anne's experience.

B He was stricter than Marilla.

C He thought that Anne should be punished for her behaviour.

D He didn't think that Anne needed to behave well.

E Matthew had no discipline himself.

COMPREHENSION

15:00
15 minutes

Read the passage below and then answer the questions that follow.

The Time Machine (by HG Wells)

In this extract, the time traveller tries out his machine for the very first time.

1   It was at ten o'clock today that the first of all Time Machines began its career. I gave it a last tap, tried all the screws again, put one more drop of oil on the quartz rod, and sat myself in the saddle. ... I took the starting lever in one hand and the stopping one in the other, pressed the first, and almost immediately the second.

5   I seemed to reel; I felt a nightmare sensation of falling; and, looking round, I saw the laboratory exactly as before. Had anything happened? For a moment I suspected that my intellect had tricked me. Then I noted the clock. A moment before, as it seemed, it had stood at a minute or so past ten; now it was nearly half-past three!

I drew a breath, set my teeth, gripped the starting lever with both hands, and went off with
10 a thud. The laboratory got hazy and went dark. Mrs. Watchett came in and walked, apparently without seeing me, towards the garden door. I suppose it took her a minute or so to traverse the place, but to me she seemed to shoot across the room like a rocket.

I pressed the lever over to its extreme position. The night came like the turning out of a lamp, and in another moment came tomorrow. The laboratory grew faint and hazy, then
15 fainter and ever fainter. Tomorrow night came black, then day again, night again, day again, faster and faster still. An eddying murmur filled my ears, and a strange, dumb confusedness descended on my mind.

I am afraid I cannot convey the peculiar sensations of time travelling. They are excessively unpleasant. ... As I put on pace, night followed day like the flapping of a black
20 wing. The dim suggestion of the laboratory seemed presently to fall away from me, and I saw the sun hopping swiftly across the sky, leaping it every minute, and every minute marking a day. ... The slowest snail that ever crawled dashed by too fast for me. The twinkling succession of darkness and light was excessively painful to the eye.

Then, in the intermittent darknesses, I saw the moon spinning swiftly through her
25 quarters from new to full, and had a faint glimpse of the circling stars. Presently, as I went on, still gaining velocity, the palpitation of night and day merged into one continuous greyness; the sky took on a wonderful deepness of blue, a splendid luminous colour like that of early twilight; the jerking sun became a streak of fire, a brilliant arch, in space; the moon a fainter fluctuating band; and I could see nothing of the stars, save
30 now and then a brighter circle flickering in the blue.

The landscape was misty and vague. I was still on the hillside upon which this house now stands, and the shoulder rose above me grey and dim. I saw trees growing and changing like puffs of vapour, now brown, now green; they grew, spread, shivered, and passed away. I saw huge buildings rise up faint and fair, and pass like dreams. ...

35 The little hands upon the dials that registered my speed raced round faster and faster.

Presently I noted that the sun belt swayed up and down, from solstice to solstice, in a minute or less, and that consequently my pace was over a year a minute; and minute by minute the white snow flashed across the world, and vanished, and was followed by the bright, brief green of spring.

40 The unpleasant sensations of the start were less poignant now. They merged at last into a kind of hysterical exhilaration. ...so with a kind of madness growing upon me, I flung myself into futurity. ... What strange developments of humanity, what wonderful advances upon our rudimentary civilisation, I thought, might not appear when I came to look nearly into the dim elusive world that raced and fluctuated before my eyes! I saw

45 great and splendid architecture rising about me, more massive than any buildings of our own time, and yet, as it seemed, built of glimmer and mist. I saw a richer green flow up the hillside, and remain there, without any wintry intermission. Even through the veil of my confusion the earth seemed very fair.

And so my mind came round to the business of stopping.

① **When he first tried it out, how did the time traveller know that his machine was working?**
- [ ] **A** The time machine disappeared.
- [ ] **B** He landed on another planet.
- [ ] **C** He had travelled backwards in time for many centuries.
- [ ] **D** The hands on the clock had moved forward several hours.
- [ ] **E** The moon went past him.

② **The author describes how Mrs Watchett 'seemed to shoot across the room like a rocket' (line 12). What is this an example of?**
- [ ] **A** Alliteration
- [ ] **B** A simile
- [ ] **C** A metaphor
- [ ] **D** Exaggeration
- [ ] **E** Personification

③ **The time traveller watches day and night passing very quickly. Which of the following does he not describe in the sky?**
- [ ] **A** The sun hopping
- [ ] **B** The moon spinning
- [ ] **C** The stars circling
- [ ] **D** A snail dashing by
- [ ] **E** A black bird flapping

④ **Which of these words is a synonym for 'luminous' (line 27)?**
- [ ] **A** Flame
- [ ] **B** Radiant
- [ ] **C** Alight
- [ ] **D** Starless
- [ ] **E** Firework

⑤ **How did the author ride the time machine?**

- [ ] **A** He sat in the cockpit.
- [ ] **B** He strapped himself to the lever.
- [ ] **C** He sat in the saddle.
- [ ] **D** He climbed into the frame.
- [ ] **E** He rode on the footplate.

⑥ **As the time traveller's trip progressed, what made him realise that he was travelling faster and faster?**

- [ ] **A** The ride became very jumpy.
- [ ] **B** The laboratory window became hazy.
- [ ] **C** The quartz rod needed oiling.
- [ ] **D** The hands on the dials raced around more quickly.
- [ ] **E** The lever went to its extreme position.

⑦ **How is this passage written?**

- [ ] **A** In the first person, past tense
- [ ] **B** In the third person, past tense
- [ ] **C** In the first person, future tense
- [ ] **D** In the passive voice
- [ ] **E** In the third person, plural

⑧ **The time traveller eventually found himself in a state of 'hysterical exhilaration' (line 41).**
How was he feeling?

- [ ] **A** He was suffering from uncontrolled fear.
- [ ] **B** He felt that he would never be able to stop the time machine.
- [ ] **C** He felt a sensation of uncontrolled elation and excitement.
- [ ] **D** His mind was facing a mad state of panic.
- [ ] **E** He knew the excitement would eventually end.

⑨ **The word 'rudimentary' (line 43) is an antonym of which of these words?**

- [ ] **A** Basic
- [ ] **B** Introductory
- [ ] **C** Advanced
- [ ] **D** Detailed
- [ ] **E** Fundamental

⑩ **'I saw the moon spinning swiftly through her quarters' (lines 24–25).**
Which part of speech is the word 'swiftly' in this clause?

- [ ] **A** Noun
- [ ] **B** Verb
- [ ] **C** Adjective
- [ ] **D** Adverb
- [ ] **E** Preposition

SPELLING

05:00
5 minutes

In these sentences there are some spelling mistakes.

In each sentence, there is either one spelling mistake or no mistake. Find the group of words with the mistake in it and circle A, B, C or D.

If there is no mistake, circle N.

① For me to be able to watch the days and months spin by was an incredable sight.
    A   B   C   D   N

② The time traveller was gripped by unusual sensaitions as he rode the machine.
    A   B   C   D   N

③ It is generelly considered by scientists to be impossible to travel through time.
    A   B   C   D   N

④ The Moon rotates on its axes around the Earth once every month.
    A   B   C   D   N

⑤ The Earth's lanscapes change considerably with the passage of millennia.
    A   B   C   D   N

⑥ Our summer and winter solstices are marked respectivally by the longest day and night.
    A   B   C   D   N

⑦ Great architects have been known to create buildings of enourmous significance.
    A   B   C   D   N

⑧ A scientist's laboratory can be the arena for amazing observations and discoveries.
    A   B   C   D   N

⑨ Over the corse of a day the sky takes on hues of cobalt, amber, turquoise and rose.
    A   B   C   D   N

⑩ As the Earth spins and the years pass, we might all be considered travellers through time.
    A   B   C   D   N

PUNCTUATION

05:00
5 minutes

In these sentences there are some punctuation mistakes.

In each sentence, there is either one punctuation mistake or no mistake. Find the group of words with the mistake in it and circle **A, B, C** or **D**.

If there is no mistake, circle **N**.

1. The hotels swimming pool had not been used all winter and needed cleaning.
   A   B   C   D   **N**

2. How many times do you need to be told to keep quiet early in the morning.
   A   B   C   D   **N**

3. He had forgotten the keys' to his house and had to go to a café for the afternoon.
   A   B   C   D   **N**

4. The cricket match was extremely exciting; both sides played the game aggressively.
   A   B   C   D   **N**

5. The dark clouds rolled in from over the hills and we knew, we needed to find cover.
   A   B   C   D   **N**

6. The homeowner put out their rubbish bin in preparation for the bin collectors: to arrive.
   A   B   C   D   **N**

7. "That fan needs batteries before it will work properly" said our friend Niko.
   A   B   C   D   **N**

8. It seemed ages before the ships' captain turned the boat around to help the others.
   A   B   C   D   **N**

9. We travelled to the show more in hope than expectation, of getting tickets.
   A   B   C   D   **N**

10. I was truly delighted to discover that I had been selected to play the lead part.
    A   B   C   D   **N**

GRAMMAR

Choose the best word, or group of words, to complete each sentence.

Circle A, B, C, D or E.

1. We usually **A) counts B) counted C) measure D) measuring E) clock** time in minutes, hours and days.

2. The moon is **A) are B) am C) our D) was E) were** nearest neighbour in space, and orbits our planet each month.

3. In days gone by, great forests **A) cover B) covered C) covert D) covering E) was covered** the land where we now live.

4. The hands on my watch **A) will B) were C) is D) are E) was** always travel in a clockwise direction.

5. My brother **A) bring B) bought C) give D) brought E) bough** me some fir cones from the forest.

6. From where we **A) will B) is C) was D) are E) were** sitting we could see all the way to a far horizon.

7. Usually, crops **A) are B) were C) where D) was E) is** planted in the spring and harvested in the late summer and autumn.

8. The traveller **A) had watched B) watch C) watching D) watcher E) see** a snail speeding along as time raced by.

9. The five senses **A) our B) were C) is D) are E) was** sight, hearing, touch, taste and smell.

10. The children were very grateful when the test **A) went B) comes C) finished D) come E) came** to an end.

THIS PAGE HAS DELIBERATELY
BEEN LEFT BLANK

COMPREHENSION AND SPELLING,

PUNCTUATION & GRAMMAR 7

Look out for Billy's tips and hints.

LEARN: READING SKILLS

Reading widely and often is really important to help improve your vocabulary and understanding of grammar.

Let's look at some key skills that will help you when you're tackling a comprehension passage.

Read the Title

You will usually be given the context of a passage, but not always. Whether you are or not, the title of the passage can help you understand quickly what is going on or being referred to. The title *The Time Machine*, for example, will help you appreciate what is being talked about in the passage.

Take Your Time

Don't read too quickly in your enthusiasm to get to the questions. It is important to 'tune in' to the text so, especially at the start, concentrate hard and go over anything that you don't quite understand.

Remember where in the text things happen or are talked about – it will be useful for the questions.

Read With Expression

Once you have read the passage through, go back and read it with expression. Throw yourself into the passage with passion. Don't just read it mechanically – read with expression, act out the parts and engage with the text. It will help significantly with your understanding.

Use your imagination – if it is a fictional story, think of the characters and plot as though you were watching a film.

Tricky Words

Don't panic if there are words that you don't understand. Read the context more than once and it should give you an idea of what the word means or what it is referring to. It can also be useful to look for clues in the questions.

Read the Questions Slowly and Carefully

Take your time over the questions. Don't rush and think you know what the question is asking – make sure you fully understand it and what answer is required.

Read Between the Lines

Sometimes the answer to a question is not explicitly stated, so you must use the clues provided to decipher the information in a text. This is called inference.

Example question 1

Clare wasn't looking where she was going and stepped into a puddle. Muddy water splashed onto her jeans. "I'm glad I wasn't wearing my white jeans," she said to her friend, Umar.

Which statement is likely to be true from the information given?

A Clare got muddy water on Umar's trousers.

B Not all of Clare's trousers are blue.

C It was raining as Clare and Umar walked.

D None of the above.

Example question 2

In some families, parents give their children weekly or monthly pocket money. Sometimes this is given in exchange for completing jobs around the house. Some children are encouraged to save some of their money – they might put it in a bank or a piggy bank.

Which statement is likely to be true from the information given?

A Pocket money is always payment for a part-time job.

B Some children don't spend their pocket money straightaway.

C Some banks won't take pocket money.

D None of the above.

Make sure you practise all forms of comprehension – fiction, non-fiction and poetry.

COMPREHENSION

Read the passage below and then answer the questions that follow.

Transformation Scene from Vice Versa (by F. Anstey)

In this comic story, a rather ill-natured father, by a sort of magical accident, gets himself turned into the perfect image of his son, whilst inwardly remaining just as he was – and the boy makes use of the same magic to turn himself into the absolute image of his father, whilst remaining wholly a boy.

1   But no sooner had Paul met the reflection in the glass than he started back in incredulous horror – then returned and stared again and again. Surely, surely, this could not be he! He had expected to see his own familiar portly bow-windowed presence there – but somehow, look as he would, the mirror insisted upon reflecting the figure of his son
5   Dick. Could he possibly have become invisible and have lost the power of casting a reflection – or how was it that Dick, and only Dick, was to be seen there?

How was it, too, when he looked round, there was the boy still sitting there? It could not be Dick, evidently, that he saw in the glass. Besides, the reflection opposite him moved when he moved, returned when he returned, copied his every gesture!

10 He turned round upon his son with angry and yet hopeful suspicion. "You, you've been playing some of your infernal tricks with this mirror, sir," he cried fiercely. "What have you done to it?"

"Done! How could I do anything to it? As if you didn't know that!"

"Then," stammered Paul, determined to know the worst, "then do you, do you mean to tell me that you can see any – alteration in me? Tell me the truth now!"

15 "I should just think I could!" said Dick emphatically. "It's very queer, but just look here," and he came up to the sideboard and placed himself by the side of his horrified father. "Why," he said with another giggle, "we're – he-he – as like as two peas!"

They were indeed; the glass reflected now two small boys, each with chubby cheeks and auburn hair, both dressed, too, exactly alike, in Eton jackets and broad white collars; the
20 only difference to be seen between them was that, while one face wore an expression of intense glee and satisfaction, the other – the one which Mr Bultitude was beginning to fear must belong to him – was lengthened and drawn with dismay and bewilderment.

"Dick," said Paul faintly, "what is all of this? Who has been taking these liberties with me?"

"I'm sure I don't know," protested Dick, "It wasn't me. I believe you did it all yourself."

25 "Did it all myself!" repeated Paul indignantly. "Is it likely I should? It's some trickery, I tell you, some villainous plot. The worst of it is," he added plaintively, "I don't understand who I'm supposed to be now. Dick, who am I?"

① **Who is Mr Bultitude (line 21)?**

- [ ] **A** Paul's friend
- [ ] **B** Dick's teacher
- [ ] **C** Paul
- [ ] **D** Paul's father
- [ ] **E** The narrator

② **Who or what causes Dick's father's transformation?**

- [ ] **A** A broken mirror
- [ ] **B** A trick
- [ ] **C** Paul
- [ ] **D** Dick
- [ ] **E** Magic

③ **What type of word is 'portly' in line 3?**

- [ ] **A** An adverb
- [ ] **B** A verb
- [ ] **C** An adjective
- [ ] **D** A noun
- [ ] **E** A pronoun

④ **What is '... the mirror insisted upon reflecting the figure of his son Dick' (lines 4–5) an example of?**

- [ ] **A** Alliteration
- [ ] **B** An idiom
- [ ] **C** Onomatopoeia
- [ ] **D** Personification
- [ ] **E** A proverb

⑤ **What colour hair do Dick and his father have?**

- [ ] **A** Black
- [ ] **B** Blond
- [ ] **C** Grey
- [ ] **D** Dark brown
- [ ] **E** Reddish-brown

⑥ **What is Dick's reaction to his father's changed appearance?**

- [ ] **A** He is horrified.
- [ ] **B** He finds it funny.
- [ ] **C** He is scared.
- [ ] **D** He is indifferent
- [ ] **E** He is cross.

⑦ **Which of these words could most accurately replace 'incredulous' (line 2)?**

☐ **A** Disbelieving

☐ **B** Furious

☐ **C** Amused

☐ **D** Relieved

☐ **E** Complete

⑧ **Why is Paul 'indignant' in line 25?**

☐ **A** Dick is a villain.

☐ **B** He thinks that Dick has deceived him and is responsible for the changed image.

☐ **C** Dick is laughing at him.

☐ **D** Dick has accused him of being the person responsible for the changed image.

☐ **E** Dick will not go to bed.

⑨ **What does Dick's father accuse him of?**

☐ **A** Plotting with a villain

☐ **B** Breaking the mirror

☐ **C** Taking liberties with him

☐ **D** Trickery

☐ **E** Becoming invisible

⑩ **What does the idiom 'as like as two peas' (line 17) mean?**

☐ **A** The father and son both like peas.

☐ **B** They both look like peas.

☐ **C** They are both green with anxiety.

☐ **D** They look alike.

☐ **E** There are peas on the sideboard.

SPELLING

In these sentences there are some spelling mistakes.

In each sentence, there is either one spelling mistake or no mistake. Find the group of words with the mistake in it and circle A, B, C or D.

If there is no mistake, circle N.

① Anyone found responsable for damaging this mirror will be severely reprimanded.
    A   B   C   D   N

② Today in gymnastics you will be required to succesfully mirror the actions of your partner.
    A   B   C   D   N

③ I believe that I look extreemely elegant in this suit: surely the mirror could not lie?
    A   B   C   D   N

④ A mirror is basicaly a piece of glass with a coating of silver or aluminium on the reverse.
    A   B   C   D   N

⑤ In the past, a reflective surface similer to glass was fashioned from polished metal.
    A   B   C   D   N

⑥ The ornate, decorative surrounding on the mirror did not paticularly appeal to his taste.
    A   B   C   D   N

⑦ If I was offered a special power, invisibility would definately be my choice.
    A   B   C   D   N

⑧ Prabhat was grateful for the oppertunity to study the fascinating art of illusion at school.
    A   B   C   D   N

⑨ The magician declared that his consience would not permit him to perform the trick.
    A   B   C   D   N

⑩ His unexpected comments were met with a humerous reaction from the audience.
    A   B   C   D   N

PUNCTUATION

 05:00 5 minutes

In these sentences there are some punctuation mistakes.

In each sentence, there is either one punctuation mistake or no mistake. Find the group of words with the mistake in it and circle **A**, **B**, **C** or **D**.

If there is no mistake, circle **N**.

① we ran as quickly as we could towards the fire, knowing time was of the essence.

    A   B   C   D   **N**

② How many people were there at the school concert this year compared to last year.

    A   B   C   D   **N**

③ The teachers, worried that the children would run off kept a very close eye on them.

    A   B   C   D   **N**

④ Lets all go to the park after school; hopefully we can see some of our friends there.

    A   B   C   D   **N**

⑤ The televisions' remote control was broken so we took it to the repair shop.

    A   B   C   D   **N**

⑥ Hopeful that the weather would improve we set out for the beach regardless.

    A   B   C   D   **N**

⑦ The best things about manchester are the fantastic transport links and restaurants.

    A   B   C   D   **N**

⑧ How many times do I have to ask you to be quiet when you enter the school?

    A   B   C   D   **N**

⑨ "Everybody needs to go to the museum at least once" said our teacher, knowingly.

    A   B   C   D   **N**

⑩ The new movie was wonderful probably the most dramatic action film I have ever seen.

    A   B   C   D   **N**

GRAMMAR

05:00
5 minutes

Choose the best word, or group of words, to complete each sentence.

Circle A, B, C, D or E.

1. We were **A) assurance B) insurance C) assured D) ascertained E) aspect** that the referee for the match would be neutral.

2. My neighbours **A) is B) and C) am D) our E) are** friendly and really interesting people.

3. The spy used **A) intelligentsia B) intelligence C) interruption D) telling E) tension** reports to lead him to the secret documents.

4. We could **A) of B) and C) is D) have E) here** chosen a different option, on reflection.

5. Every cloud **A) have B) hand C) has D) heard E) hits** a silver lining.

6. We **A) where B) wear C) were D) would E) will** all hoping to pass the exams.

7. Before going on holiday, we **A) encased B) enclosed C) insured D) ensured E) entranced** that all our windows were locked.

8. The rules were **A) supposed B) supposition C) support D) super E) supplement** to ensure that a fair game took place.

9. It was one of **A) are B) ear C) hare D) here E) our** biggest regrets that we didn't take more holidays together.

10. She was thirsty, so she **A) drinks B) drink C) drank D) dank E) dark** some water.

THIS PAGE HAS DELIBERATELY
BEEN LEFT BLANK

COMPREHENSION AND SPELLING,

PUNCTUATION & GRAMMAR 8

Look out for Billy's tips and hints.

LEARN: POETRY

As well as fiction and non-fiction passages, you may be presented with a poem in the comprehension test.

You might think that poems are trickier than fiction or non-fiction, but with plenty of practice you will soon be able to tackle poetry comprehensions confidently.

How to Approach the Task

- **Read the poem more than once**

  You are unlikely to be familiar with the poem that you are presented with. Take your time and read through the poem first. Do not worry about understanding every word or even verse. Just read through it once to get the general gist (idea) of what the poem is about.

  Now think about what you have just read. Ask yourself what is happening and what the poem is about – what the poet is trying to get across.

  Having formulated your thoughts, read the poem again at least twice. Slow down at points you don't immediately understand; see if they become clearer in the context of the whole poem and what you think is happening.

- **Read the poem aloud in your head**

  Well, not actually aloud – you don't want to disturb your classmates! The point of doing this is that most poems use language and rhythms to make the poem more interesting for the reader. Watch out for rhyming schemes and alliteration in particular.

Typical Questions – Key Poetry Terms

- **Rhyming scheme**

  You will often be asked to give the rhyming scheme for a particular poem.

  Rhyming schemes are straightforward once you understand how they work. Look for the lines in a verse that rhyme and attach the right letter to them (A, B, C, D, and so on).

  For example: If the rhyming lines in a verse are line 1 with 3 (lay, day) and line 2 with 4 (kit, fit), the rhyming scheme would be ABAB.

  > ### Example question 1
  >
  > What is the rhyming scheme in this poem?
  >
  > The big hairy cat
  > Was stuck on the mat
  > Whilst the clever old dog
  > Was sitting on the log

- **Alliteration**

  As seen on pages 38–39, alliteration is a common literary technique used in poetry to add fun and rhythm. It involves the repetition of the same sounds.

  <u>Example question 2</u>

  Give one example of alliteration from this verse.

  The snake hid in the long grass
  Cruel and cunning
  Ready to pounce on its prey

- **Stanza**

  A group of lines in a poem make up a stanza.

  Different types of stanzas are named based on the number of lines they contain.

Type of stanza	Number of lines
Tercet	3
Quatrain	4
Quintain	5
Sestet	6
Septet	7
Octave	8

The rhythm and language of a poem is usually very important. Read as many poems as possible in your spare time!

COMPREHENSION

15:00
15 minutes

Read the poem below and then answer the questions that follow.

My Shadow (by Robert Louis Stevenson)

1   I have a little shadow that goes in and out with me,

And what can be the use of him is more than I can see.

He is very, very like me from the heels up to the head;

And I see him jump before me, when I jump into my bed.

5   The funniest thing about him is the way he likes to grow –

Not at all like proper children, which is always very slow;

For he sometimes shoots up taller like an india-rubber ball,

And he sometimes gets so little that there's none of him at all.

He hasn't got a notion of how children ought to play,

10 And can only make a fool of me in every sort of way.

He stays so close beside me, he's a coward you can see;

I'd think shame to stick to nursie as that shadow sticks to me!

One morning, very early, before the sun was up,

I rose and found the shining dew on every buttercup;

15 But my lazy little shadow, like an arrant sleepy-head,

Had stayed at home behind me and was fast asleep in bed.

1　**What is the rhyming scheme of this poem?**

☐　**A**　There isn't one.

☐　**B**　ABAB

☐　**C**　AABB

☐　**D**　ABBA

☐　**E**　ABBB

2　**What does the narrator think the use of the shadow is?**

☐　**A**　To protect him

☐　**B**　To mimic him

☐　**C**　To follow him wherever he goes

☐　**D**　To embarrass him

☐　**E**　He has no idea.

3　**Which type of word is 'before' as it is being used in line 4?**

☐　**A**　Noun

☐　**B**　Preposition

☐　**C**　Adverb

☐　**D**　Verb

☐　**E**　Adjective

4　**Why would the narrator's shadow have got larger and smaller so quickly?**

☐　**A**　It would change as the narrator grew.

☐　**B**　It would depend on the angle of the light causing the shadow.

☐　**C**　It would depend on how big the shadow wanted to look.

☐　**D**　It would depend on how much danger the narrator was in.

☐　**E**　It is impossible to tell.

5　**Which word is most similar in meaning to 'notion' as it is used in line 9?**

☐　**A**　Note

☐　**B**　Ambition

☐　**C**　Idea

☐　**D**　Notorious

☐　**E**　Plan

6　**What causes the narrator to think his shadow is a coward?**

☐　**A**　Because he won't protect him

☐　**B**　Because he is always so close to him

☐　**C**　Because he won't reveal who he really is

☐　**D**　We are not told.

☐　**E**　Because he picks on the narrator

⑦ **Which literary device is being used in line 12?**

- [ ] **A** Alliteration
- [ ] **B** Idiom
- [ ] **C** Metaphor
- [ ] **D** Onomatopoeia
- [ ] **E** Personification

⑧ **Who or what would 'nursie' have been? (line 12)**

- [ ] **A** A doctor
- [ ] **B** Medicine
- [ ] **C** A friend of the narrator
- [ ] **D** The narrator's parent
- [ ] **E** Someone who looked after the narrator

⑨ **Why would the shadow really have behaved as it did in the last verse?**

- [ ] **A** Because it was so tired
- [ ] **B** Because it was mean
- [ ] **C** It is impossible to tell.
- [ ] **D** Because the sun wasn't up
- [ ] **E** Because the narrator had grown up

⑩ **Which of these is an accurate description of a theme of this poem?**

- [ ] **A** Fear
- [ ] **B** Curiosity
- [ ] **C** Serenity
- [ ] **D** Humour
- [ ] **E** Acceptance

SPELLING

05:00
5 minutes

In these sentences there are some spelling mistakes.

In each sentence, there is either one spelling mistake or no mistake. Find the group of words with the mistake in it and circle **A, B, C** or **D**.

If there is no mistake, circle **N**.

① We were all disapointed that the party had to end earlier than originally planned.
   A   B   C   D   N

② We took separate taxis to the cricket match because there were to many of us.
   A   B   C   D   N

③ They returned from there trip with a harrowing tale of having been in danger.
   A   B   C   D   N

④ The thieves escaped from the building by rushing down the old escalater in the hall.
   A   B   C   D   N

⑤ We soon discovered that the appropriate attire for the gathering was actually informal.
   A   B   C   D   N

⑥ Hopefully, lessons will be learned and we can apreciate how fortunate we are.
   A   B   C   D   N

⑦ The teacher incorrectly assumed that we had all done our homework on Wenesday.
   A   B   C   D   N

⑧ The other team were only marginaly better than us, so we took heart from that.
   A   B   C   D   N

⑨ We particulary enjoyed visiting the theatre during our school trip as it was fascinating.
   A   B   C   D   N

⑩ She had anticipated the response from her friend and was not suprised at all.
   A   B   C   D   N

PUNCTUATION

05:00
5 minutes

In these sentences there are some punctuation mistakes.

In each sentence, there is either one punctuation mistake or no mistake. Find the group of words with the mistake in it and circle **A**, **B**, **C** or **D**.

If there is no mistake, circle **N**.

1. Does anyone know what time we are supposed to be at school on the last day of term.

   | A | B | C | D | N |

2. The potatoes' in the bag had been purchased at the massive supermarket in town.

   | A | B | C | D | N |

3. The friends absolutely soaked from the sudden storm, ran into the house to get dry.

   | A | B | C | D | N |

4. "We need to hide behind the rock over there" said Jimi, trying to sound composed.

   | A | B | C | D | N |

5. At the shop we bought tomatoes, grapes, kitchen roll, some cat food and a new mop.

   | A | B | C | D | N |

6. The library was absolutely packed I decided to work on my assignment at home instead.

   | A | B | C | D | N |

7. The cat prowled around the garden, swishing it's tail frantically as birds flew overhead.

   | A | B | C | D | N |

8. "Haven't we all done enough now to make sure that the concert goes without a hitch?"

   | A | B | C | D | N |

9. The field had been freshly, mowed; it was a beautiful sight and gave off a lovely smell.

   | A | B | C | D | N |

10. "Watch out for that large rock over there; it is so difficult to see!" Shouted Carrie.

    | A | B | C | D | N |

GRAMMAR

05:00
5 minutes

Choose the best word, or group of words, to complete each sentence.

Circle A, B, C, D or E.

1. They **A) had B) was C) were D) would E) are** be more wary of strangers in the future.

2. My computer **A) is B) as C) are D) our E) when** more powerful than my friend's.

3. The birdsong **A) wake B) wakes C) woke D) when E) went** me up early yesterday morning.

4. The chef **A) presumed B) prepared C) propel D) prevented E) prediction** her ingredients.

5. Many books **A) have B) hinge C) has D) hook E) help** a plot twist.

6. Some **A) person B) people C) group D) him E) her** don't like to take risks.

7. The parents could not **A) condone B) concern C) develop D) click E) convince** their child's bad behaviour.

8. Limited **A) suppose B) replies C) supplies D) success E) retreat** were available to the encircled soldiers.

9. She **A) implored B) deplored C) imposed D) impressed E) improvised** them to change their mind.

10. She was hungry, so **A) eat B) eats C) ate D) and E) easy** a delicious meal.

**THIS PAGE HAS DELIBERATELY
BEEN LEFT BLANK**

COMPREHENSION AND SPELLING,

PUNCTUATION & GRAMMAR 9

Look out for Billy's tips and hints.

LEARN: NON-FICTION COMPREHENSIONS

Some comprehension passages are non-fiction. They come from a factual piece rather than an imagined story. Examples of non-fiction are a newspaper article, diary extract and biographical/autobiographical text.

Newspaper Articles

Newspaper articles are set out in columns and have a main headline, which gives the reader the main point of the story. A sub-heading includes further detail. The first paragraph of a newspaper article usually summarises what happened, who was involved and where the action took place. The rest of the article gives further details about how and why it happened, often with quotes from witnesses or people involved. Newspaper articles often include at least one captioned image.

Diary Extracts

Diary extracts are written in the first person (from the author's perspective) and are a narrative of events which occur in that person's life. They describe things that have happened in chronological order and the writer includes a description of their thoughts and feelings about them.

Biographies and Autobiographies

Biographies and autobiographies are factual texts about the life of a well-known person. They appeal to readers who would like to hear about the life of that person. A biography is written about someone else, whereas an autobiography is authored by the person themselves.

What to Look Out For in Non-fiction Comprehensions

Non-fiction comprehensions are all about the retrieval and understanding of information. There are unlikely to be any characters to follow and understand, but the passage will have a topic that is being discussed and you need to thoroughly absorb all the information and understand what you are being told.

The Answer will Always be in the Text

In a non-fiction comprehension, the text will give you the answer to a question. It may not always be a simple retrieval exercise, but even with the tougher questions the text will point you in the right direction of the answer.

Consider this passage.

Chris was 12 years old, 59 years younger than his grandfather. They both loved to go to football matches to support their local club.

Example question 1 (straight retrieval)

How old was Chris?

A 12

B 59

C 71

D 13

E 14

This is a straight retrieval question – you can read the answer directly in the text.

Example question 2 (logical retrieval)

How old was Chris's grandfather?

A 47

B 59

C 61

D 71

E 95

Although you can't read the answer directly in the text, the information is given for you to work it out. You will never have to guess – there will always be clues in the text for you to answer the question.

Don't be put off by what may look like a complex or dense non-fiction passage. Just remember – the answers will always be there.

COMPREHENSION

15:00
15 minutes

Read the passage below and then answer the questions that follow.

An All-round Great Game

1 Nothing is more fun than a game of marbles with a friend. I have spent many a happy
   hour lying spread-eagled on the floor or hunched cross-legged as I played for 'keepsies',
   aiming to win for myself some of my friend's prized 'onionskins', although sadly, I no
   longer play. I cannot claim to be a 'mibologist' (an expert in marbles), but I do know that
5 a 'taw' is what is needed to target a 'mib'. If that is news to you, read on and learn all
   about these spherical toys which, for very little cost, can provide you with hours of fun
   as well as being objects of beauty that you can enjoy beholding.

   Where marbles originated is a mystery, but they have been around for a very long time
   and are one of the most favourite nostalgic toys. A very long time ago, when marbles
10 were first being used, they were handmade in a variety of ways and from all kinds of
   materials including stones (such as agate), ivory, clay, glass or even wood. The game is
   thought to be one of the oldest in the world and there are many examples of marbles
   from Greek, Roman, Egyptian and Native American excavation sites. In the poem 'Nux',
   by the Roman poet Ovid, there is reference to walnuts being used to play marbles.

15 In 1844, Sam Dyke of Akron, Ohio, invented a method that made it possible for his
   factory to mass produce marbles, making one million clay marbles each day. Nowadays,
   marbles are mostly made from glass. Mass production of them began in 1915 after the
   invention of another machine. This one worked so well that the marbles that you can
   buy today are made in more or less the same way.

20 The aim of a game of marbles is relatively simple; knock as many of your opponents'
   marbles (mibs) as possible out of the circle. However, there is a whole new vocabulary
   that you must learn when playing marbles. When your hand (at least one knuckle on
   the ground) is in what you think is the correct position to shoot your marble, you are
   'knuckled down'. If you cross the line of the circle on your shot (a minor form of cheating),
25 you could be accused of 'fudging'. 'Playing for keepsies' means that any competitors'
   marbles that you knock out of the ring are yours to keep, and many tears were shed upon
   this occurrence when I was a child. I wonder if the saying 'losing your marbles' originates
   from the game of marbles? Losing my 'gobby' (large marble) was a tragedy!

   Several names refer to the marble's size. Just a few of the names for any marble bigger than the
30 majority are a 'bonker', 'shooter', 'thumper', 'smasher', 'boulder', 'bumboozer', 'toebreaker', or
   'hogger'. A 'taw' is the name given to one of these larger marbles when it is being used to shoot
   at smaller marbles. 'Ducks' are marbles to be shot at. The idiom 'to get your ducks in a row' is
   reputed to originate from the game of pool in which a ball in front of a pocket, an easy shot, is
   sometimes called a 'duck'. Surely then, pool is related to the game of marbles?

35 There are hundreds of games that can be played with marbles, but the most common one
   used for modern tournament play (yes, you can actually compete in the British and World
   Marbles Championship!) is known as 'Ringer'. In this game, 13 'ducks' are arranged in the

shape of a cross in the centre of a ring by two mibsters. Mibsters take turns knuckling down with their shooters and firing into the ducks with the aim of shooting them out of
40 the ring. Points are tallied. When a shooter stays in the ring, the mibster can keep shooting until it leaves the ring, thus procuring extra turns until their shooter leaves the ring. Each duck removed scores a point and play repeats in further rounds until someone reaches the winning score of 50. Playing 'keepsies' is, of course, a bonus.

My heart still longs to play the game again, but my aged knees find the prospect
45 unattractive. Maybe you should have a go and give people like me the chance to enjoy watching. One last word of warning: Don't let youngsters below the age of three get their hands on your marbles, as to them they could pose great danger.

① **Which of these facts about marbles is correct?**
      A   They are cheap to buy.
      B   They are unobtainable in the UK.
      C   They are expensive to buy.
      D   They are free in toy shops.
      E   They are only sold in America.

② **Which of these materials are not mentioned in the text as being used to make marbles?**
      A   Agate
      B   Ivory
      C   Clay
      D   Wood
      E   Metal

③ **What type of word is 'spread-eagled' in line 2?**
      A   A noun
      B   An adjective
      C   An adverb
      D   A verb
      E   A preposition

④ **In the poem 'Nux', what are used as marbles?**
      A   Hazelnuts
      B   Pine cones
      C   Walnuts
      D   Blackberries
      E   Chestnuts

⑤ **When marbles were first mass produced, what were they made from?**

- **A** Glass
- **B** Stone
- **C** Clay
- **D** Marble
- **E** Plastic

⑥ **If a player is found to have been 'fudging' in a game, what is likely to happen to them?**

- **A** They will never be allowed to play marbles again.
- **B** They will feel very proud.
- **C** They will miss a turn.
- **D** They will win the game.
- **E** The game will have to end with no winner.

⑦ **What is the phrase 'losing your marbles' an example of?**

- **A** A proverb
- **B** An instruction
- **C** A tongue twister
- **D** An idiom
- **E** A command

⑧ **Who or what is a 'mibster'?**

- **A** An enormous marble
- **B** The name of a marbles game
- **C** A player in a marbles game
- **D** The loser in a marbles game
- **E** The winner in a marbles game

⑨ **What is the most likely reason that the writer no longer plays marbles?**

- **A** Getting up and down from the floor is difficult.
- **B** They can't afford any marbles.
- **C** They have forgotten how to play.
- **D** They have knobbly knees.
- **E** Their parents won't let them play.

⑩ **Why does the passage advise you to keep your marbles away from young children?**

- **A** They might hide them.
- **B** They might throw them and break something.
- **C** They won't know what to do with them.
- **D** They might beat you in a game.
- **E** They might choke on them.

SPELLING

05:00
5 minutes

In these sentences there are some spelling mistakes.

In each sentence, there is either one spelling mistake or no mistake. Find the group of words with the mistake in it and circle **A, B, C** or **D**.

If there is no mistake, circle **N**.

1. You needed a valid excuce in order to miss the end-of-term awards presentation.
   A   B   C   D   N

2. She managed to successfully achieve the required pass mark in her examnations.
   A   B   C   D   N

3. The animals rampaged through the jungle, desperately looking for something to eat.
   A   B   C   D   N

4. Nobody was discouraged by the inclement whether; they were on holiday after all.
   A   B   C   D   N

5. Although the trip had been uneventfull, it had been an arduous journey to complete.
   A   B   C   D   N

6. The dog retreived the ball every time it was hurled by its owner across the park.
   A   B   C   D   N

7. Although the instructions seemed simple enough, we still strugled to get it started.
   A   B   C   D   N

8. Some metals are precious, expensive to aquire and much sought after as a result.
   A   B   C   D   N

9. The cricket coach lambasted her players for not putting in sufficient effort in training.
   A   B   C   D   N

10. The doctor always tried to see as many patience as she could during the day.
    A   B   C   D   N

PUNCTUATION

05:00
5 minutes

In these sentences there are some punctuation mistakes.

In each sentence, there is either one punctuation mistake or no mistake. Find the group of words with the mistake in it and circle **A**, **B**, **C** or **D**.

If there is no mistake, circle **N**.

1. "Let's go to Marble Falls for our holiday this year," suggested Mum. "It'll be fun"
   A   B   C   D   N

2. Joan said that "she'd like her fingernails to be marbled next time they were manicured.
   A   B   C   D   N

3. I saw a stunningly beautiful rare marbled gecko when I was in Queensland, Australia.
   A   B   C   D   N

4. The friendly, Alsatian dog offered me his ball, clearly wanting me to play throw and catch.
   A   B   C   D   N

5. The gumball's were tempting me, but I knew that they weren't good for my teeth.
   A   B   C   D   N

6. In sport, the smallest ball used is a squash ball: the largest is a basketball, I believe.
   A   B   C   D   N

7. I kicked what appeared to be a football; it was made of concrete, and I collapsed in tears.
   A   B   C   D   N

8. What on earth can be the tiny, soft, little balls in my spinach soup and will they harm me?
   A   B   C   D   N

9. Both mine and my two friends marble patterns were exactly the same. Wasn't that cool?
   A   B   C   D   N

10. Although we were trying hard, the problem was annoyingly taking us round in circles.
    A   B   C   D   N

GRAMMAR

05:00
5 minutes

Choose the best word, or group of words, to complete each sentence.

Circle A, B, C, D or E.

① We **A) take B) took C) look D) like E) turn** everything from the fridge before it was turned off.

② The lion had a **A) vicious B) viscous C) voracious D) valid E) vibrating** appetite.

③ The poor weather **A) predicted B) pronoun C) prevailed D) provoked E) prevented** the match from starting on time.

④ She was **A) presumed B) perturbed C) precious D) protractor E) perfume** by the strange noises from the cupboard.

⑤ The man was **A) arrowed B) alarmed C) regulated D) arrogant E) arbitrary** and thought a lot of himself.

⑥ The **A) patron B) passion C) passed D) invoke E) devote** of our teacher was very compelling.

⑦ We were **A) elected B) debated C) developed D) demoted E) delighted** that our friend had returned from abroad.

⑧ The **A) sustainability B) susceptibility C) attain D) contain E) stain** of fishing is a controversial issue.

⑨ We **A) ascertain B) assessed C) aspect D) acclaimed E) aggravated** our options and decided to go first.

⑩ There was plenty of food at the **A) singular B) rumbustious C) sumptuous D) scarce E) barren** buffet.

THIS PAGE HAS DELIBERATELY BEEN LEFT BLANK

COMPREHENSION AND SPELLING,

PUNCTUATION & GRAMMAR 10

LEARN: SENTENCE STRUCTURES

Types of Sentence Structure

There are three main types of sentence structure: simple, compound and complex. Remember that all sentences contain a subject and a verb.

- A **simple sentence** contains one single piece of information.

  For example: He doesn't like vegetables.

- A **compound sentence** contains two simple sentences joined together with a conjunction.

  For example: He doesn't like vegetables but he does like meat. The conjunction in this sentence is 'but'.

- A **complex sentence** starts with a conjunction and has more than one piece of information that is separated by a comma.

  For example: Although he doesn't like vegetables, Sam loves to eat meat and salad.

  #### Example question 1

  Write a compound sentence using this information.

  Karl is 21. He has never travelled abroad.

  #### Example question 2

  Write a complex sentence using this information.

  Bhavna plays cricket. She isn't an accomplished catcher.

Types of Sentence

The three common types of sentence are command, interrogative and exclamatory.

- **Command sentences** give instructions. They often start with a verb.

  For example: Turn the light off before you go to bed.

- **Interrogative sentences** are questions, so they end with a question mark.

  For example: What time will you be turning the light off?

- **Exclamatory sentences** include strong feelings or emotions, so they end with an exclamation mark.

  For example: That building is on fire!

Example question 3

What type of sentence is this?

That goal in the last minute was incredible!

Example question 4

What type of sentence is this?

How many minutes were on the clock when that goal was scored?

Expanded Noun Phrases

An expanded noun phrase adds more detail to a noun by adding at least one adjective.

For example: The massive blue whale was in the middle of the ocean.

In this example, 'the massive blue whale' is the expanded noun phrase.

Example question 5

Identify the expanded noun phrase in this sentence.

The boy enjoyed eating some colourful sweets.

Using good grammar and different sentence types will make your writing interesting to read and make it flow well.

COMPREHENSION

15:00
15 minutes

Read the passage below and then answer the questions that follow.

Windsor Castle

1   If you are ever lucky enough to visit Windsor, you will find yourself beneath the ramparts of the oldest and largest inhabited castle in the world. It is possible that you will see, flying from the top of the Round Tower, the Royal Standard. This majestic flag shows everyone that the monarch is in residence.

5   Elizabeth II, who died in 2022, was one of 40 monarchs who have called Windsor Castle home for nearly 1000 years, since the Norman invasion of England in 1066 by William the Conqueror. Interestingly, even they were not the first inhabitants; centuries before that, the Saxons had named the place Windlesora, which means 'a riverbank with a windlass'.* Their kings had had a much smaller settlement beside the Thames in what is now called Old Windsor.

10   **William the Conqueror's Wooden Keep**

William's castle was built in the 11th century when he was establishing a line of defensive fortifications around London. The site he chose was located on a hill, within an easy 20-mile march from London, still conveniently positioned on the River Thames, which at the time (long before trains or motorways) was a vital medieval route through England.

15   The first building constructed on the site was a wooden structure known as a keep, which is a fortified tower set on the top of a man-made mound, and protected by an outer wall.

St George's Chapel

This beautiful Gothic building stands inside the Lower Ward of Windsor Castle. Construction of the chapel began in 1475 by Edward IV. It was completed in 1528 under

20   the reign of Henry VIII. The chapel is the resting place for 10 former monarchs, including Henry VIII, Charles I, George III, Edward VII and George V. Queen Victoria and her husband Albert are buried nearby at The Royal Mausoleum at Frogmore. St George's Chapel is also the burial site for Queen Elizabeth II.

Edward III and The Order of the Garter

25   Every June, the Garter Day procession takes place at Windsor Castle, accompanied by a marching band and Knights of the Order who attend alongside the monarch and the royal family, wearing grand ceremonial robes.

The Most Noble Order of the Garter, founded by King Edward III in 1348, was established to commemorate an unfortunate event at a ball the king was hosting.

30   One story says that Edward was dancing with his partner when suddenly her blue garter** dropped to the floor! All the bystanders laughed at the embarrassed lady. However, Edward was a gallant king; he picked up the garter and admonished the courtiers in French, with the words "Honi soit qui mal y pense!"*** At this, the other guests realised that they had not been courteous.

35   The king inaugurated the Order of the Garter with a great feast and joust, and the phrase "Honi soit qui mal y pense" remains its motto to this day.

Windsor Castle – Past, Present and Future

Despite its long history, the Windsor Castle we see today is to all intents and purposes a 19th-century creation (less than 200 years old). During this time many of the outside
40 walls were remodelled and even the Round Tower was made taller! The skyline was designed to be dramatic when seen from a distance or silhouetted against the horizon, a romantic image of tall towers and battlements influenced by the fashion of the time and what the 19th-century architects thought a castle of legend should be like.

In truth, every monarch has marked their time on the place; built dungeons, added
45 chapels, frescoes on the ceilings and, most recently, after a terrible fire in 1992, rebuilt damaged rooms to look more like they would have done in much earlier times.

So if you are ever lucky enough to visit Windsor, and find yourself beneath the ramparts of the oldest and largest inhabited castle in the world, remember its history but also allow yourself to wonder what changes will come over the next thousand years .... If you
50 were the next monarch, how would you leave your mark on this fascinating building?

Note:
*   *A windlass is a winch – a device for hauling and lifting large objects.*
**   *A garter is a narrow band of fabric worn around the leg to keep stockings up.*
***   *In modern English "Honi soit qui mal y pense" is popularly translated as "Evil to him who thinks evil".*

① **What does the Royal Standard flying from the top of the Round Tower signify?**

- **A** That a royal event is taking place in Windsor.
- **B** That the monarch is staying at Windsor Castle.
- **C** There is a strong wind blowing.
- **D** It reminds us about the ancient history of the place.
- **E** All of the above.

② **What is the best synonym for the word 'monarch'?**

- **A** Leader
- **B** King
- **C** Queen
- **D** Sovereign
- **E** President

③ **The passage describes William the Conqueror 'establishing a line of defensive fortifications around London' (lines 11–12). What is the closest explanation of this?**

- **A** He was building a fortress in London.
- **B** His army was fighting outside London.
- **C** He was building defences in places surrounding the capital.
- **D** He didn't want to be in London, preferring Windsor.
- **E** He thought the Queen might attack.

④ **In the passage, why was the River Thames so important to the early kings?**

☐ **A** It was the best travel and trade route through the country in those days.

☐ **B** The early kings enjoyed travelling by boat.

☐ **C** The river was a vital way of defending their armies from enemies.

☐ **C** The river provided them with fish, an important source of food.

☐ **E** It provided the population with drinking water.

⑤ **How long did it take to build St George's Chapel?**

☐ **A** Over 100 years

☐ **B** Less than 50 years

☐ **C** More than 50 years

☐ **D** The reign of two kings

☐ **E** Between 100 and 150 years

⑥ **Place these events in the correct order.**

1 **King Edward inaugurated The Order of the Garter.**

2 **The lady's garter fell down.**

3 **The courtiers were ashamed.**

4 **The lady was embarrassed.**

5 **King Edward uttered the words "Honi soit qui mal y pense".**

☐ **A** 1, 3, 2, 5, 4

☐ **B** 1, 2, 4, 3, 5

☐ **C** 2, 3, 4, 5, 1

☐ **D** 2, 4, 5, 3, 1

☐ **E** 2, 4, 3, 1, 5

⑦ **'The skyline was designed to be dramatic when seen from a distance' (lines 40–41).**
Which part of speech is the word 'dramatic'?

☐ **A** Noun

☐ **B** Verb

☐ **C** Preposition

☐ **D** Adverb

☐ **E** Adjective

8 **How did Windsor Castle change in the 19th century?**
1 **The Round Tower was heightened.**
2 **The walls were redesigned.**
3 **The dungeon was built.**
4 **Frescoes were painted on ceilings.**
5 **Rooms were restored.**

- **A** 1 and 2
- **B** 1 and 5
- **C** 2 and 3
- **D** 1 and 4
- **E** 3 and 4

9 **How do you think the author expects the castle to change in the next thousand years?**

- **A** Future kings will be responsible for its decline.
- **B** Every monarch will add something of their own to the castle.
- **C** The castle will remain the same in the future.
- **D** The ramparts will require extensive modernisation.
- **E** More monarchs will be buried there.

10 **What type of writing is this text?**

- **A** A historical narrative
- **B** Historical fiction
- **C** An information text
- **D** A diary
- **E** A report

SPELLING

05:00
5 minutes

In these sentences there are some spelling mistakes.

In each sentence, there is either one spelling mistake or no mistake. Find the group of words with the mistake in it and circle **A, B, C** or **D**.

If there is no mistake, circle **N.**

1 One of William's finest acomplishments was the wooden keep at Windsor.
   |___A___|___B___|___C___|___D___| N

2 The anchient name for the town, given by the Saxons, was Windlesora.
   |___A___|___B___|___C___|___D___| N

3 The castle could not be siezed by attackers because of its strong ramparts.
   |___A___|___B___|___C___|___D___| N

4 Knights of old were famed for their chivalry and bravery in the face of battle.
   |___A___|___B___|___C___|___D___| N

5 Throughout history, arguements have raged over lands, kingdoms and religion.
   |___A___|___B___|___C___|___D___| N

6 During a ball, a lady was ofended when courtiers laughed at her mishap.
   |___A___|___B___|___C___|___D___| N

7 From miles around, the romantic outline of Windsor Castle is very noticable.
   |___A___|___B___|___C___|___D___| N

8 The king and his courtiers used to persue deer through Windsor Great Park.
   |___A___|___B___|___C___|___D___| N

9 After the Norman invasion, William the Conqueror desided to build many fortifications.
   |___A___|___B___|___C___|___D___| N

10 Royal palaces often have ornate tapestries on the walls and highly decorated cielings.
   |___A___|___B___|___C___|___D___| N

PUNCTUATION

05:00
5 minutes

In these sentences there are some punctuation mistakes.

In each sentence, there is either one punctuation mistake or no mistake. Find the group of words with the mistake in it and circle A, B, C or D.

If there is no mistake, circle N.

1. Windsor Castle stands above the thames twenty miles from London.

   A   B   C   D | N |

2. A lady was embarrassed when her blue garter fell to the floor?

   A   B   C   D | N |

3. A flag called the Royal Standard flies from the castle when the monarch is in residence

   A   B   C   D | N |

4. "Where should I build a fortress?" Asked King William as he marched with his army.

   A   B   C   D | N |

5. Windsor Great Park is where monarchs hunted deer, hares, fowl, and other creatures.

   A   B   C   D | N |

6. Honi soit qui mal y pense," announced King Edward to his courtiers at the ball.

   A   B   C   D | N |

7. Over the centuries, every monarch has left their mark on the castle.

   A   B   C   D | N |

8. Queen Elizabeth II found Windsor's Castle an attractive and comfortable home.

   A   B   C   D | N |

9. The dungeons at Windsor were built to imprison enemies of the monarch!

   A   B   C   D | N |

10. The king jumped into the moat before, his boat sank and swam to safety.

    A   B   C   D | N |

GRAMMAR

05:00
5 minutes

Choose the best word, or group of words, to complete each sentence.

Circle A, B, C, D or E.

1. Windsor Castle has been the setting for many historic, royal **A) times B) occasions C) scene D) landmarks E) themes**.

2. If you visit Windsor, you will **A) found B) fine C) find D) fin E) fly** yourself near the castle.

3. William I built the castle when he **A) is B) wasn't C) did D) was E) will** establishing fortresses around London.

4. The Changing of the Guard is something to **A) watching B) watched C) look out D) watch E) look** when you visit Windsor.

5. At the time, the River Thames **A) is B) was C) will be D) were E) where** a vital route through the country.

6. Windsor Castle **A) has been B) was C) will be D) always was E) is** home to kings and queens for centuries.

7. By the time your trip is over, you will **A) have B) of C) has D) not E) off** seen many historical sights.

8. The Most Noble Order of the Garter **A) was B) is C) were D) would E) wasn't** established by King Edward III in 1348.

9. If you had a choice, how **A) did B) do C) wood D) does E) would** you leave your mark on Windsor Castle?

10. Queen Victoria and her husband Prince Albert **A) is B) was C) are D) here E) wear** buried at The Royal Mausoleum at Frogmore.

ANSWERS

Answers

COMPREHENSION AND SPELLING, PUNCTUATION & GRAMMAR 1

Learn: Word Types (pages 8–9)

Example question 1: vibrating

Example question 2: sadly

Example question 3: abstract noun

Example question 4: proper noun

Example question 5: towards

Comprehension: *A Letter Home* (pages 10–12)

Question	Answer	Explanation
1.	C	He is fighting in a war: *trenches*, *enemy shells* (lines 2 and 3)
2.	B	He claims they had regular food, were safe and got post.
3.	A	*stately* is an adjective
4.	E	We are not told. Robert doesn't actually know and is just guessing.
5.	B	To make sure Robert wasn't revealing any war secrets: 'I am not allowed to tell you about our operations in my letters…' (line 8)
6.	C	A newspaper
7.	D	West London, like Robert
8.	D	We can tell from the context that it was because the lawns were so large.
9.	A	To ration food supply
10.	C	Hardly

Spelling (page 13)

Question	Answer	Explanation
1.	A	difficult
2.	D	athletes
3.	N	
4.	B	accustomed
5.	N	
6.	D	trepidation
7.	B	orchestra
8.	C	whether
9.	C	practised
10.	C	competition

Punctuation (page 14)

Question	Answer	Explanation
1.	A	A comma is needed after *back*.
2.	B	An apostrophe is needed to show possession: *farmer's*.

3.	D	This is a question, so it needs a question mark at the end rather than a full stop.
4.	B	The word *it's* shouldn't have the apostrophe: *its*.
5.	C	A comma is needed after *midday*.
6.	N	
7.	C	A comma is needed after *road*.
8.	C	The comma needs removing after *know*.
9.	D	The apostrophe needs removing in *lots'*.
10.	B	A lower case 'e' is needed in the word *Exclaimed*.

Grammar (page 15)

Question	Answer	Explanation
1.	D	weren't
2.	D	too
3.	B	believe
4.	B	doesn't
5.	B	was
6.	C	weather
7.	A	decided
8.	C	legislation
9.	E	would
10.	C	are

COMPREHENSION AND SPELLING, PUNCTUATION & GRAMMAR 2

Learn: Punctuation (pages 18–19)

Example question 1: The sun, having come out from behind the clouds, gave off a dazzling glare.

Example question 2: The building is on fire!

How many lessons do we have this afternoon?

The road is quite long.

Example question 3: There are three types of triangles: isosceles, equilateral and scalene.

Example question 4: The car had broken down; Joe decided to walk home.

Comprehension: *The Problem of Plastic in our Oceans* (pages 20–22)

Question	Answer	Explanation
1.	E	It can't be destroyed.
2.	C	*Waterborne chemicals* (line 4)
3.	A	
4.	B	When humans eat the contaminated fish
5.	D	
6.	C	There is no time to waste – 'it is time for action' (line 14).

7.	D	'There are other items we can buy instead that do not cause such a problem' (line 16).
8.	A	Almost all offer recycling facilities for plastics.
9.	D	They look for volunteers.
10.	E	It is intended to motivate you into taking action.

Spelling (page 23)

Question	Answer	Explanation
1.	A	Witch
2.	B	travels
3.	A	trusty
4.	D	musical
5.	A	accused
6.	A	course
7.	A	ascent
8.	N	
9.	B	hoping
10.	B	peculiar

Punctuation (page 24)

Question	Answer	Explanation
1.	A	*Its* should have an apostrophe because it is a contraction of *It is*.
2.	B	*Aunt* should be capitalised because it refers to a particular aunt.
3.	D	The question mark should be replaced by a full stop.
4.	D	A full stop should be added at the end of the sentence.
5.	B	*Museums* is a plural word, so the apostrophe showing possession should come after the 's' (*museums'*).
6.	C	A hyphen is needed for the noun *grown-up*.
7.	N	
8.	C	A question mark should be added after *lies*.
9.	D	*Bridge* should not have a capital letter.
10.	A	*Hotels* is a plural word, so the apostrophe showing possession should come after the 's' (*hotels'*).

Grammar (page 25)

Question	Answer	Explanation
1.	D	anything
2.	C	most
3.	C	watched
4.	D	direction

5.	B	evade
6.	C	presume
7.	E	should've
8.	A	forward
9.	B	whereas (*whereas* means in comparison with another fact)
10.	A	did it (the simple past tense agrees with the verb *cried*)

COMPREHENSION AND SPELLING, PUNCTUATION & GRAMMAR 3

Learn: Spelling Skills (pages 28–29)

Example question 1: Child's own answer, for instance: **S**u eats **i**n **z**oos **e**verywhere.

Example question 2: Child's own answers but they might include: thief, chief, receive

Example question 3: Child's own answers but they might include: eight, neighbour, sleigh

Example question 4: Child's own answers but they might include: fry, fried; cry, cried; terrify, terrified

Example question 5: Child's own answers but they might include: fly, flyer

Comprehension: *Boudicca* (pages 30–32)

Question	Answer	Explanation
1.	E	Humility is not a concrete thing.
2.	C	In this context, *cause* is a noun meaning *beliefs*.
3.	D	Line 5 says that history allows us to 'comprehend our present'. To comprehend means to understand.
4.	D	To be conciliatory means to pacify or calm a person or situation. The idiom is a figurative way of saying the same thing.
5.	B	*Infuriated* has its root in the word 'fury', which means anger. Boudicca wanted revenge so she must have been very angry.
6.	B	Lines 34–35 tell us that we can learn from her 'refusal to bow meekly to injustice'. To stick up for yourself has the same meaning.
7.	C	Line 10 says that the Roman laws allowed inheritance 'only through the male line'. This excludes any other answer.
8.	D	Line 28 cites 'an inferior quality of weaponry' as the cause. Inferior means lower in quality.
9.	E	In the context of this quotation, the word *legend* is referring to wanting to be well known and do amazing things.
10.	D	Line 27 informs us that the layer is soot. Soot is created by fire.

Spelling (page 33)

Question	Answer	Explanation
1.	D	whipped
2.	C	striking
3.	B	endeavour
4.	D	heroes

5.	B	one
6.	C	past
7.	N	
8.	C	women's
9.	C	breaker
10.	C	souls

Punctuation (page 34)

Question	Answer	Explanation
1.	A	The word *they* should start with a capital 't'.
2.	D	The sentence should end with a question mark.
3.	D	A full stop needs adding at the end of the sentence.
4.	A	The comma needs removing.
5.	C	The apostrophe needs removing: the word should be *its*.
6.	D	The comma should be removed after *drinks*.
7.	B	*Pointed* shouldn't have a capital 'p'.
8.	A	The apostrophe isn't in the correct place; the word should be *teacher's*.
9.	D	The exclamation mark isn't needed at the end of the sentence.
10.	A	The apostrophe isn't needed: the word should be *walls*.

Grammar (page 35)

Question	Answer	Explanation
1.	C	under
2.	D	must have
3.	B	accepted
4.	E	is
5.	A	determined
6.	E	them
7.	B	although
8.	C	too
9.	D	keen
10.	C	that

COMPREHENSION AND SPELLING, PUNCTUATION & GRAMMAR 4

Learn: Literary Devices (pages 38–39)

Example question 1: as cold as ice

Example question 2: drowning in it

Example question 3: Squirrels searched for supplies.

Example question 4: squeaked; bang

Example question 5: spilled the beans

Comprehension: *The Golden Touch* (pages 40–42)

Question	Answer	Explanation
1.	C	Line 1 states that 'Midas was enjoying himself in his treasure-room, one day, as usual'.
2.	E	Lines 7–8 describe how 'Certainly, although his figure intercepted the sunshine, there was now a brighter gleam upon all the piled-up treasures than before'.
3.	A	Saw
4.	D	Lines 11–12 explain that 'Midas knew that he had carefully turned the key in the lock, and that no mortal strength could possibly break into his treasure-room'.
5.	A	Adjective (it is describing the tone)
6.	C	Simile
7.	D	Lines 27–29 state that '"I have done pretty well,—pretty well," answered Midas, in a discontented tone. "But, after all, it is but a trifle, when you consider that it has taken me my whole life to get it together.'
8.	D	Enormous
9.	B	A myth
10.	C	Lines 46–47 tell the reader what King Midas wishes: "… I wish everything that I touch to be changed to gold!" This has disastrous consequences when the young visitor grants the wish to him.

Spelling (page 43)

Question	Answer	Explanation
1.	D	treasure-room
2.	A	precious
3.	B	creatures
4.	B	occasions
5.	A	careful
6.	N	
7.	D	visible
8.	D	greedy
9.	C	prized
10.	N	

Punctuation (page 44)

Question	Answer	Explanation
1.	C	The 'a' of *are* should be capitalised despite being within a sentence, because it's at the beginning of direct speech.
2.	C	Incorrect use of possessive apostrophe: the word should read *jewels*.

3.	C	After the question mark, *Asked* shouldn't have a capital 'a'.
4.	D	The comma should be removed after *Lesbos*.
5.	N	
6.	B	The full stop after *man* should be changed to a comma; a full stop isn't needed before *King* just because it starts with a capital letter.
7.	C	*East* shouldn't have a capital 'e'.
8.	A	There is a missing opening bracket before the word '*my*'.
9.	D	There is a missing possessive apostrophe: the word should be *oceans'*.
10.	N	

Grammar (page 45)

Question	Answer	Explanation
1.	C	distracted
2.	D	past
3.	E	compelling
4.	B	should
5.	E	astute
6.	A	belated
7.	E	marginally
8.	B	willing
9.	B	way
10.	E	wait

COMPREHENSION AND SPELLING, PUNCTUATION & GRAMMAR 5

Learn: Grammar (pages 48–49)

Example question 1: running

Example question 2: tall

Example question 3: slowly

Example question 4: unless

Example question 5: onto

Example question 6: us

Example question 7: Jamie

Example question 8: grass

Example question 9: imagination

Comprehension: *A Technical Marvel* (pages 50–52)

Question	Answer	Explanation
1.	E	She is six times older than Emma.
2.	D	
3.	C	

4.	C	For being ungrateful and not embracing the modern era
5.	D	'Tap tap tap'
6.	C	Lines 13–14 say "...they are obsessed with their phones."
7.	D	It had been warped by the rain.
8.	C	
9.	E	It was all too familiar to them.
10.	D	

Spelling (page 53)

Question	Answer	Explanation
1.	A	devastated
2.	B	glowing
3.	B	business
4.	B	enthusiastic
5.	C	professor
6.	B	confessed
7.	D	expedition
8.	A	disappointed
9.	N	
10.	A	surprised

Punctuation (page 54)

Question	Answer	Explanation
1.	C	A question mark is needed after *park*.
2.	D	A question mark is needed after *booked*.
3.	C	A comma needs adding after *could*.
4.	A	There is a missing possessive apostrophe: the word should be *Johnson's*.
5.	A	The apostrophe needs removing from *footballer's*: the word should be *footballers*.
6.	N	
7.	C	The semi-colon should be removed.
8.	N	
9.	B	The comma should be removed.
10.	C	A comma needs adding after *manager*.

Grammar (page 55)

Question	Answer	Explanation
1.	D	is
2.	B	has
3.	E	would

4.	C	went
5.	B	trying
6.	A	came
7.	B	so
8.	E	proved
9.	C	catching
10.	C	because

COMPREHENSION AND SPELLING, PUNCTUATION & GRAMMAR 6

Learn: Retrieval and Inference Comprehension Questions (pages 58–61)

Example question 1: **E** The text says it was 'for reasons best known to herself'.

Example question 2: **A** The text says she watched over Anne 'with a keen eye'.

Example question 3: **C** The text says that 'by noon she had concluded that Anne was smart and obedient'.

Example question 4: **B** She describes Anne's behaviour as dreadful and criticises Matthew for taking her side.

Example question 5: **A** Matthew was more understanding and lenient towards Anne. He feared that Marilla would punish her too harshly, perhaps not even feeding her.

Comprehension: *The Time Machine* (pages 62–64)

Question	Answer	Explanation
1.	D	Lines 6–8 state 'Had anything happened? For a moment I suspected that my intellect had tricked me. Then I noted the clock. A moment before, as it seemed, it had stood at a minute or so past ten; now it was nearly half-past three!'
2.	B	Simile, because the comparison word *like* is used.
3.	E	A black bird flapping
4.	B	Radiant is a synonym of luminous, which means bright or glowing.
5.	C	Lines 1–3 state: 'I gave it a last tap, tried all the screws again, put one more drop of oil on the quartz rod, and sat myself in the saddle'.
6.	D	Line 35 says: 'The little hands upon the dials that registered my speed raced round faster and faster'.
7.	A	The author is also the main character, using the pronouns *I*, *me* and *my*. The verb forms are in the past, for example *was*, *gave*, *saw*, and so on.
8.	C	'Hysterical exhilaration' implies that he feels out of control, but elated and excited at what is happening.
9.	C	*Rudimentary* means basic or simple.
10.	D	*Swiftly* describes how the moon is spinning. *Spinning* is a verb, and adverbs describe verbs.

Spelling (page 65)

Question	Answer	Explanation
1.	D	incredible
2.	C	sensations
3.	A	generally
4.	B	axis
5.	A	landscapes
6.	C	respectively
7.	D	enormous
8.	N	
9.	A	course
10.	N	

Punctuation (page 66)

Question	Answer	Explanation
1.	A	There is a missing possessive apostrophe: the word should be *hotel's*.
2.	D	A question mark needs adding after *morning*.
3.	B	The apostrophe should be removed at the end of *keys'*: the word should be *keys*.
4.	N	
5.	C	The comma needs removing.
6.	D	The colon needs removing.
7.	C	A comma needs adding after *properly*.
8.	B	The apostrophe is in the wrong place: the word should be *ship's*.
9.	C	The comma needs removing.
10.	N	

Grammar (page 67)

Question	Answer	Explanation
1.	C	measure
2.	C	our
3.	B	covered
4.	A	will
5.	D	brought
6.	E	were
7.	A	are
8.	A	had watched
9.	D	are
10.	E	came

COMPREHENSION AND SPELLING, PUNCTUATION & GRAMMAR 7

Learn: Reading Skills (pages 70–71)

Example question 1: **B**

Example question 2: **B**

Comprehension: *Transformation Scene from Vice Versa* (pages 72–74)

Question	Answer	Explanation
1.	C	When Paul and Dick were both reflected in the mirror, Mr Bultitude was 'beginning to fear' that the other must be him.
2.	E	The introduction to the text explains that the incident is caused by 'a sort of magical accident'.
3.	C	*Portly* describes Paul's presence, a noun, so the word must be an adjective.
4.	D	*Insisted* is a verb meaning 'to demand forcefully'. As this is something done by humans, then the mirror is being personified.
5.	E	The images in the mirror have auburn hair. Auburn is a reddish-brown colour.
6.	B	Line 17 says "Why," he [Dick] said with another giggle, "we're – he-he…".
7.	A	*Incredulous* means *disbelieving*. Paul cannot believe that the image he is seeing is not his own.
8.	D	Dick suggests that Paul "did it all yourself" (line 24). Paul's indignant response in line 25 is "Is it likely I should?"
9.	D	In lines 10–11, Paul says "You, you've been playing some of your infernal tricks with this mirror…"
10.	D	When two people are likened to peas in a pod, it means that they look identical.

Spelling (page 75)

Question	Answer	Explanation
1.	A	responsible
2.	C	successfully
3.	B	extremely
4.	A	basically
5.	B	similar
6.	C	particularly
7.	C	definitely
8.	B	opportunity
9.	B	conscience
10.	C	humorous

Punctuation (page 76)

Question	Answer	Explanation
1.	A	The lower case 'w' in *we* should be a capital letter.
2.	D	A question mark is needed after *year*.
3.	C	A comma is needed after *off*.
4.	A	*Lets* should be *Let's*.
5.	A	The apostrophe is in the wrong place: the word should be *television's*.
6.	B	A comma is needed after *improve*.
7.	B	The lower case 'm' in *manchester* should be a capital letter.
8.	N	
9.	C	A comma is needed after *once*.
10.	B	A semi-colon or dash is needed after *wonderful*.

Grammar (page 77)

Question	Answer	Explanation
1.	C	assured
2.	E	are
3.	B	intelligence
4.	D	have
5.	C	has
6.	C	were
7.	D	ensured
8.	A	supposed
9.	E	our
10.	C	drank

COMPREHENSION AND SPELLING, PUNCTUATION & GRAMMAR 8

Learn: Poetry (pages 80–81)

Example question 1: Look at the lines that rhyme: lines 1 and 2 (cat, mat) and lines 3 and 4 (dog, log). So the rhyming scheme of this poem is AABB.

Example question 2: The answer could be 'Cruel and cunning' or 'pounce on its prey', as both examples have repeating sounds.

Comprehension: *My Shadow* (pages 82–84)

Question	Answer	Explanation
1.	C	
2.	D	Line 10 says, 'And can only make a fool of me in every sort of way.'
3.	B	
4.	B	The narrator doesn't know it, but it would be the angle of the light.
5.	C	
6.	B	It is always so close behind him.

7.	A	It is alliteration – *shame, shadow, stick, sticks*
8.	E	
9.	D	There would have been no shadow present, so the narrator thought it had stayed in bed.
10.	B	

Spelling (page 85)

Question	Answer	Explanation
1.	A	disappointed
2.	D	too
3.	B	their
4.	D	escalator
5.	N	
6.	C	appreciate
7.	D	Wednesday
8.	B	marginally
9.	A	particularly
10.	D	surprised

Punctuation (page 86)

Question	Answer	Explanation
1.	D	A question mark is needed after *term*.
2.	A	The apostrophe needs removing so that the word reads *potatoes*.
3.	A	A comma is needed after *friends*.
4.	C	A comma is needed after *there*.
5.	N	
6.	B	A semi-colon is needed after *packed*.
7.	C	*It's* should be *its*.
8.	N	
9.	B	The comma needs removing after *freshly*.
10.	D	The capital 's' in *Shouted* should be lower case: *shouted*.

Grammar (page 87)

Question	Answer	Explanation
1.	D	would
2.	A	is
3.	C	woke
4.	B	prepared
5.	A	have
6.	B	people

7.	A	condone
8.	C	supplies
9.	A	implored
10.	C	ate

COMPREHENSION AND SPELLING, PUNCTUATION & GRAMMAR 9

Learn: Non-fiction Comprehensions (pages 90–91)

Example question 1: **A** Chris was 12.

Example question 2: **D** Chris's grandfather was 71.

Comprehension: *An All-round Great Game* (pages 92–94)

Question	Answer	Explanation
1.	A	Line 6 says that marbles can be obtained 'for very little cost'.
2.	E	Marbles could be made of metal, but the possibility is not mentioned in the text.
3.	C	*Spread-eagled* is a compound word describing the verb *lying*. It is therefore an adverb.
4.	C	Lines 13–14 say that in the poem 'Nux' 'there is reference to walnuts being used to play marbles'.
5.	C	Mass-produced marbles were first made of clay (see line 16), and later glass.
6.	C	The text says that *fudging* is a minor form of cheating. The most usual penalty for this in a game is to miss a turn.
7.	D	'To lose your marbles' is an idiom. It means to become insane.
8.	C	When the game is described (paragraph 6), the person doing all the actions is called the mibster. A mibster must therefore be a player.
9.	A	The writer says in lines 43–44 that their 'aged knees find the prospect unattractive'. So we can conclude that they find up and down movements challenging.
10.	E	Small pieces such as marbles are a choking hazard for children.

Spelling (page 95)

Question	Answer	Explanation
1.	B	excuse
2.	D	examinations
3.	N	
4.	C	weather
5.	B	uneventful
6.	A	retrieved
7.	C	struggled
8.	B	acquire

9.	N	
10.	C	patients

Punctuation (page 96)

Question	Answer	Explanation
1.	D	A full stop is needed after *fun*.
2.	A	Incorrect addition of opening speech marks; not required for indirect speech.
3.	B	Commas are needed after *beautiful* and *rare*.
4.	A	The comma is not needed after *friendly*.
5.	A	The apostrophe needs removing so that the text reads *gumballs*.
6.	C	The colon should be a semi-colon; a semi-colon joins two independent clauses.
7.	N	
8.	C	A comma is needed after *soup*.
9.	B	An apostrophe should be added after the 's' of *friends* to show possession.
10.	N	

Grammar (page 97)

Question	Answer	Explanation
1.	B	took
2.	C	voracious
3.	E	prevented
4.	B	perturbed
5.	D	arrogant
6.	B	passion
7.	E	delighted
8.	A	sustainability
9.	B	assessed
10.	C	sumptuous

COMPREHENSION AND SPELLING, PUNCTUATION & GRAMMAR 10

Learn: Sentence Structures (pages 100–101)

Example question 1: Karl is 21, but he has never travelled abroad.

Example question 2: Although Bhavna plays cricket, she isn't an accomplished catcher.

Example question 3: Exclamatory sentence

Example question 4: Interrogative sentence

Example question 5: some colourful sweets

Comprehension: *Windsor Castle* (pages 102–105)

Question	Answer	Explanation
1.	B	The Royal Standard flies above whatever palace the monarch is staying in.
2.	D	*Sovereign* is the closest synonym to *monarch*, as it can mean either a king or queen.
3.	C	The defensive fortifications were forts or castles protecting London but built outside the capital (for example, a 20-mile march from London).
4.	A	The passage states that the river was a vital medieval route through England.
5.	C	According to the passage, construction started in 1475 and was completed in 1528, which is 53 years.
6.	D	2, 4, 5, 3, 1
7.	E	*Dramatic* is an adjective describing the skyline of Windsor Castle.
8.	A	1 and 2. None of the other improvements were made in the 19th century, according to the passage.
9.	B	Lines 49–50 ask: 'If you were the next monarch, how would you leave your mark on this fascinating building?' This implies that the author expects future monarchs to add something of their own to the castle.
10.	C	It's an information text.

Spelling (page 106)

Question	Answer	Explanation
1.	B	accomplishments
2.	A	ancient
3.	B	seized
4.	N	
5.	B	arguments
6.	B	offended
7.	D	noticeable
8.	B	pursue
9.	C	decided
10.	D	ceilings

Punctuation (page 107)

Question	Answer	Explanation
1.	B	The word '*thames*' should have a capital 't'.
2.	D	The question mark should be a full stop.
3.	D	The full stop is missing.
4.	C	The 'A' in *Asked* should be lower case.

5.	C	The comma needs removing after *fowl*.
6.	A	The opening speech marks are missing.
7.	N	
8.	B	The apostrophe and 's' need removing so the word reads *Windsor*.
9.	D	The exclamation mark should be a full stop.
10.	B	The comma should be removed.

Grammar (page 108)

Question	Answer	Explanation
1.	B	occasions
2.	C	find
3.	D	was
4.	D	watch
5.	B	was
6.	A	has been
7.	A	have
8.	A	was
9.	E	would
10.	C	are

Marking Chart

Fill in the tables below with your results from each section.

Comprehension and Spelling, Punctuation & Grammar 1

Comprehension	/10	Spelling	/10	Punctuation	/10	Grammar	/10

Comprehension and Spelling, Punctuation & Grammar 2

Comprehension	/10	Spelling	/10	Punctuation	/10	Grammar	/10

Comprehension and Spelling, Punctuation & Grammar 3

Comprehension	/10	Spelling	/10	Punctuation	/10	Grammar	/10

Comprehension and Spelling, Punctuation & Grammar 4

Comprehension	/10	Spelling	/10	Punctuation	/10	Grammar	/10

Comprehension and Spelling, Punctuation & Grammar 5

Comprehension	/10	Spelling	/10	Punctuation	/10	Grammar	/10

Comprehension and Spelling, Punctuation & Grammar 6

Comprehension	/10	Spelling	/10	Punctuation	/10	Grammar	/10

Comprehension and Spelling, Punctuation & Grammar 7

Comprehension	/10	Spelling	/10	Punctuation	/10	Grammar	/10

Comprehension and Spelling, Punctuation & Grammar 8

Comprehension	/10	Spelling	/10	Punctuation	/10	Grammar	/10

Comprehension and Spelling, Punctuation & Grammar 9

Comprehension	/10	Spelling	/10	Punctuation	/10	Grammar	/10

Comprehension and Spelling, Punctuation & Grammar 10

Comprehension	/10	Spelling	/10	Punctuation	/10	Grammar	/10

Progress Grid

Colour these charts with your total score from each section to see how well you have done.

Comprehension and Spelling, Punctuation & Grammar 1

1	2	3	4	5	6	7	8	9	10	11	12	13	14	15	16	17	18	19	20	21	22	23	24	25	26	27	28	29	30	31	32	33	34	35	36	37	38	39	40

Comprehension and Spelling, Punctuation & Grammar 2

1	2	3	4	5	6	7	8	9	10	11	12	13	14	15	16	17	18	19	20	21	22	23	24	25	26	27	28	29	30	31	32	33	34	35	36	37	38	39	40

Comprehension and Spelling, Punctuation & Grammar 3

1	2	3	4	5	6	7	8	9	10	11	12	13	14	15	16	17	18	19	20	21	22	23	24	25	26	27	28	29	30	31	32	33	34	35	36	37	38	39	40

Comprehension and Spelling, Punctuation & Grammar 4

1	2	3	4	5	6	7	8	9	10	11	12	13	14	15	16	17	18	19	20	21	22	23	24	25	26	27	28	29	30	31	32	33	34	35	36	37	38	39	40

Comprehension and Spelling, Punctuation & Grammar 5

1	2	3	4	5	6	7	8	9	10	11	12	13	14	15	16	17	18	19	20	21	22	23	24	25	26	27	28	29	30	31	32	33	34	35	36	37	38	39	40

Comprehension and Spelling, Punctuation & Grammar 6

1	2	3	4	5	6	7	8	9	10	11	12	13	14	15	16	17	18	19	20	21	22	23	24	25	26	27	28	29	30	31	32	33	34	35	36	37	38	39	40

Comprehension and Spelling, Punctuation & Grammar 7

1	2	3	4	5	6	7	8	9	10	11	12	13	14	15	16	17	18	19	20	21	22	23	24	25	26	27	28	29	30	31	32	33	34	35	36	37	38	39	40

Comprehension and Spelling, Punctuation & Grammar 8

1	2	3	4	5	6	7	8	9	10	11	12	13	14	15	16	17	18	19	20	21	22	23	24	25	26	27	28	29	30	31	32	33	34	35	36	37	38	39	40

Comprehension and Spelling, Punctuation & Grammar 9

1	2	3	4	5	6	7	8	9	10	11	12	13	14	15	16	17	18	19	20	21	22	23	24	25	26	27	28	29	30	31	32	33	34	35	36	37	38	39	40

Comprehension and Spelling, Punctuation & Grammar 10

1	2	3	4	5	6	7	8	9	10	11	12	13	14	15	16	17	18	19	20	21	22	23	24	25	26	27	28	29	30	31	32	33	34	35	36	37	38	39	40

Read the statements below for some hints and tips.

1–15: Re-read the Learn section and have another go at the questions.

16–29: Good effort! Have another go at the questions you got wrong.

30–40: Well done! Keep up the good work.